For Sid
Bw

one small plot of heaven

BOOKS BY ELISE BOULDING

The Underside of History: A View of Women Through Time

From a Monastery Kitchen

Handbook of International Data on Women (co-author)

Children's Rights and the Wheel of Life

The Social System of the Planet Earth (co-author)

Women and the Social Costs of Economic Development:
Two Colorado Case Studies (co-author)

Building a Global Civic Culture:
Education for an Interdependent World

one small plot

REFLECTIONS ON FAMILY LIFE
BY A QUAKER SOCIOLOGIST

of heaven

Elise Boulding

Pendle Hill Publications
Wallingford, Pennsylvania

One Small Plot of Heaven
Reflections on Family Life by a Quaker Sociologist

Printed in the United States of America
by Thomson-Shore, Inc., Dexter, Michigan

Book design by Carol Trasatto
Cover art by Samie Decker

Library of Congress Cataloging-in-Publication Data
will be found at the end of this book.

The essays included in this book originally appeared as follows,
and are reprinted with permission of the publishers:

Children and Solitude
Pendle Hill Pamphlet 125. Pendle Hill Publications, 1963.

The Personhood of Children and the Flight from Relationship
The Personhood of Children. 1975 Rufus Jones Lecture.
Friends General Conference, 1976.

Born Remembering
Pendle Hill Pamphlet 200. Pendle Hill Publications, 1975.

Friends Testimonies in the Home
Pamphlet. Friends General Conference, 1952.

Families as Centers of Peace and Love: Paradoxes and Contradictions
In *Friends Face the World: Continuing and Current Concerns.* Edited by
Leonard Kenworthy. Friends United Press, 1986.

Quaker Foremothers as Ministers and Householders
"Mapping the Inner Journey of Quaker Women." In *The Influence of
Quaker Women on American History.* Edited by Carol and John Stoneburner.
Studies in Women and Religion, vol. 21. The Edwin Mellen Press, 1986.

The Challenge of Nonconformity:
Reweaving the Web of Family Life for Lesbians and Gays
Friends Journal, October 1987, pages 16-18.

The Family as a Practice Ground in Making History
The Friendly Woman, Fall 1979, pages 3-6.

The Re-creation of Relationship, Interpersonal and Global
Pamphlet. The Wider Quaker Fellowship, Friends World Committee
for Consultation, 1981.

The Family as a Small Society
1982 Schumacher Lecture. E.F. Schumacher Society of America (Box 76,
RD 3, Great Barrington, MA 01230), 1982.

The Family as a Way into the Future
Pendle Hill Pamphlet 222. Pendle Hill Publications, 1978.

The greatest gift our children can give us is a capacity to see the world anew. Parents gain increased awareness if they allow their children to be their teachers.

—Friends Testimonies in the Home

Russell Boulding of the Peaceable Press in Bloomington, Indiana, eldest son of the author, suggested the book's organization and did a first edit of the entire manuscript.

Contents

Introduction

Put off the garb of woe, let mourning cease;
Today we celebrate with solemn mirth,
The planting in the ravaged waste of earth
Of one small plot of heaven, a Home of peace,
Where love unfeigned shall rule, and bring increase,
And pure eternal joy shall come to birth
And grow, and flower, that neither drought nor dearth
Shall wither, till the Reaper brings release.

Guard the ground well, for it belongs to God;
Root out the hateful and the bitter weed,
And from the harvest of thy Heart's good seed
The hungry shall be fed, the naked clad,
And love's infection, leaven-like, shall spread
Till all creation feeds from heavenly bread.

- Kenneth Boulding, "Sonnet for a Quaker Wedding"

One small plot of heaven! What a presumptuous title for a book about family life in a time when the very word "family" often evokes pain—the memories of divorce battles, bitter custody disputes, physical violence, alienating step-family relationships. Today, as it has many times in the past, the family is bearing the brunt of a major social transition—from the preindustrial to the postindustrial order. Riding out transitions has been the family's task through the centuries, on all continents, in all cultures. It multiplies its forms as it adapts to stress and strain, but it survives. It not only survives, it produces children who

1

carry on the adventure of living—sometimes cheerfully, sometimes with great imagination and daring, sometimes fearfully, sometimes angrily.

Is the human race doomed to mere survival (if that), never to rise to the heights of its own potentialities? Not as long as we can envision the development of humanity's unseen resources and be empowered by our visions. If we are looking for a starting place for both envisioning and working on everyday realities for a better future, the family can be such a starting place. Not the only place, but a good place.

I have found it so in my own life. This collection of essays is really the record of my own discoveries about family life over the years from young adulthood to the present, as a wife, mother, sociologist, peace activist—and Quaker. Mine has been a protected life, and the essays certainly reflect the safe middle-class social environment a professorial family inhabits. But they also reflect a never-ending struggle to reach out to the wider world, to make the family count as an actor in that world and in its shaping.

I met my husband-to-be, Kenneth Boulding, in the spring of 1941, at the very gathering at which I was taken into membership by the Religious Society of Friends (Quakers). During our whirlwind courtship (sedately conducted at subsequent Quaker gatherings) I caught glimpses of a new understanding of what family might mean in an era when war clouds were shadowing the world. Not yet twenty-one, I was overwhelmed by Kenneth's idea that through our marriage we were to found a colony of heaven. In that summer before our marriage, I had the awed feeling that I had somehow to reconstruct myself to be a person worthy of such a venture. I was so unready! The summer was already programmed. I was enrolled in a civilian training program for women, designed to ready us for service in war-torn areas of Europe. At the training camp I struggled to prepare myself for the double task of marriage and community service. I prayed a lot. Could I be ready in time? I know now, at age sixty-eight, that one is never ready for the next step in life's journey. We learn what we need to know on the road itself.

In joining the Society of Friends that spring forty-six years ago, I committed myself to becoming a peacemaker. But I didn't know very much about peacemaking. Kenneth Boulding, ten years older, served as a teacher-companion-guide. Entering the marriage, we both saw our task as creating a home of peace from which to help build a more peaceful world. When the impatiently awaited babies finally started coming in 1947, the practice of peace in the home became more difficult and challenging than when there were only two of us. But we knew we had to practice at home what we wanted for the world.

I first began writing about our attempts to integrate peacemaking in the home with peacemaking in the world during a summer at Pendle Hill* in 1951, while I was expecting our third child. "Friends Testimonies in the Home" was the result. That essay, revised and shortened, is the fifth in this book. I have been writing on the subject ever since, and the eleven later essays included here reflect what I have learned in the intervening decades, with five children and a husband—and now fifteen grandchildren—as teachers. Our marriage began with a very traditional division of labor between husband and wife, a division of labor with which we were both very comfortable in the 1940s. Because ideas that we took for granted then about how women should allocate their time seem strange today, I have modified "Friends Testimonies" to allow for the fact that relatively few women are full-time homemakers today. In the 1940s, most of us were housewives and wanted it that way. Core family values have remained the same, but the patterns of work inside and outside the home have changed. So have patterns of relationship, with increasing numbers of recombined families, single-parent families, and same-sex couples. How I have learned to see each of these patterns as belonging within the definition

*Pendle Hill is a Quaker center for study and contemplation located near Philadelphia, Pennsylvania.

of "family," even to the point of including the live-alone householder in that definition, is described in the course of these writings.

The essays are not arranged chronologically, but rather thematically into three sections. **Children and Growing Up** includes three essays based on my own experience with our children and their friends as well as on my sociological studies; one of these is an autobiographical essay about my own "growing up" (a still-continuing process). This section also includes some poems written at a special time in my life for our grandchildren, poems which my eldest son insists belong here!

"Children and Solitude," published in 1963 as a Pendle Hill Pamphlet, gives the grounds for my convictions about the personhood of children and the quality of their social being. My own observations of deep spiritual awareness in our five children from their earliest years, and the importance of solitude in their inner maturation, spurred me to seek further evidence in the records of childhood memories to be found in Quaker journals. This pamphlet was written at a time when our own children were growing into adolescence and taking on more complex social roles. I was eager to capture the immediacy of the earlier childhood openness to stirrings of the spirit. I can still remember thinking, as I prepared to write this essay, "I must do it now—I mustn't wait, or I will forget what these early years have been like!"

"The Personhood of Children and the Flight From Relationship" was written as the 1976 Rufus Jones Lecture for Philadelphia Yearly Meeting. It brings together different strands of family experience and personal reflection, and records my observations of how children are everywhere marginalized in contemporary society. Categorization as "child" excludes them from partnership in our thinking and in our doing. In our own Quaker community in Ann Arbor, Michigan, I witnessed the energy and imagination that come into a social group when children are included, made partners with us.

"Born Remembering" was published as a Pendle Hill Pamphlet in 1975. What I learned from our children about the fruits of solitude bore rich harvest when I entered my own year of solitude the year our youngest went away to college. "Born Remembering" is a kind of spiritual autobiography, and is the only essay that includes memories of my own childhood. My struggles to be responsive to the inner call, family duties, intellectual tasks, and social-action demands came to a head in my early fifties. Writing about those struggles during my hermit's year helped me sort them out. While not in a formal sense an essay about family life, it is probably as much about what family means in the living of a life as anything I have written. Since many people ask me what that hermit's year means in my life today, I have written a short postscript answering that question.

"Songs for Our Grandchildren from Hermitage Hollow" includes part of a letter and several poems from a booklet I prepared for my grandchildren in 1976, shortly after the year of solitude ended. In solitude, one's family becomes very vivid and precious. Ever since that year, hermitage time has been family reconnecting time—with Kenneth, with the children and their spouses, with the grandchildren—as I think about and pray for each of them. I hope these poems give a flavor of the sense of closeness to loved ones that can come with the experience of solitude.

Quaker Family Life includes my first effort to capture in writing what family life is about for Quakers, as well as my most recent assessment of where we are as a pacifist community in relation to peace building in the family. It also contains a historical study of Quaker foremothers and the problems they faced as homemakers and ministers, and an examination of the important contributions Quaker gay and lesbian couples make to the Society of Friends and to society at large.

"Friends Testimonies in the Home," originally written in 1951, required a lot of reflection and revision. I have tried to keep intact the mission of family life based on the images of God as parent and Jesus as elder brother, with spouses as helpmeets under divine guidance—concepts that were and still are very vivid to me—in a way that remains authentic in light of more recent understandings about the cultural constraints of patriarchy. The Christian heritage is my context for working at Quaker practice in the family, especially in the face of contrary external pressures.

Rereading the section on nonconformity made me realize how much more "conformed to this world" Quakers have become over the past thirty-five years. I have let most of the original stand as a reminder of our call to nonconformity. Rereading the section on worship in the home, I similarly realized how much more secular we have become in that same period. How to carry on authentic family worship in daily rhythm was one of my most central concerns as our children were growing up. I won't say that family worship has become anachronistic today, but it no longer gets the attention it used to. What does this mean? While I have shortened that section, I have left enough to convey the quality of the original concern.

"Families of Centers of Peace and Love: Paradoxes and Contradictions" is an essay that appears in abridged form in Leonard Kenworthy's *Friends Face the World: Continuing and Current Quaker Concerns* (1987). It takes a sober look at the discrepancy between what we Friends say we are trying to do and what we actually do. Violence finds its way even into the homes of peacemakers. Yet facing these problems becomes the basis for dealing with violence in the larger society. We cannot do abroad what we have not learned to do at home.

"Quaker Foremothers as Ministers and Householders" is excerpted from a study I did in 1980 for a Quaker history project organized by Carol and John Stoneburner of Guilford College (later published as a volume entitled *The Influence of Quaker Women on American History*). I include it because the study produced such unexpectedly rich material on the family life of some remarkable women who were led into public life in the early decades of Quakerism. The tension between a strong spiritual calling to travel in the ministry and the demands of family life—with or without the added claims of small children—comes out clearly in the journals kept by these women. Reading their words, though the language is unfamiliar and archaic, we discover that such tensions are not unique to our own times. The importance of their inward spiritual lives in maintaining a balance between conflicting callings is a necessary reminder to us today that the inner life is the anchor for the outer.

"The Challenge of Nonconformity: Reweaving the Web of Family Life for Lesbians and Gays" appeared in *Friends Journal* in 1987. Several years after the hermitage time, I chose to commute between our home in Boulder, Colorado, and Hanover, New Hampshire, so I could teach at Dartmouth College. By this time our children all had their own homes and Kenneth was turning retirement into an adventurous series of visiting professorships. At Dartmouth, I became acquainted for the first time with the gay and lesbian community, and the struggles of gay couples to be accepted as families—along with struggles to be accepted by their own families. As I came to know more about the gay witness in the Society of Friends, I realized that we had new teachers among us—and that the concept of family was taking on still another dimension. This essay may be hard for some readers to digest. It is offered as food for thought.

Family and Society includes four relatively recent essays on the theme of the family as a miniature society and as a shaper of the larger society, including the global society.

"The Family as a Practice Ground in Making History" first appeared in 1979 in a Quaker periodical called *The Friendly Woman*. Written after all our children were married and I myself was teaching at Dartmouth, it was an attempt to recapture the sense that had been with me so strongly while our children were growing up—that everything we did as a family mattered for the world. Whether it was backyard play, camping experiences, or demonstrations and other public witnesses, it was all part of an apprenticeship for larger social-change tasks. Whatever we did locally was a metaphor for claiming responsibility for the state of the planet.

"The Re-creation of Relationship, Interpersonal and

Global" was a pamphlet published in 1981 by the Wider Quaker Fellowship. It sounds the theme that has been so central in my life—the linking of interpersonal relationships in family and community with the globe-spanning relationships needed to create a world at peace. My years of association with the Tokyo-based United Nations University as well as with UNESCO brought new dimensions of that linkage to my awareness. This essay was written just at the time when I was preparing for the first workshop of what has now become a major enterprise, the Imaging a World Without Weapons Project. One of the most affirming aspects of this project for me personally has been that over and over again, with many different groups of people in many different social and cultural settings, imagery has emerged from these workshops of strong "familistic" local communities linked globally by a variety of imagined communication and collaboration devices.

"The Family as a Small Society" was the 1982 Schumacher Lecture, and was published by the E.F. Schumacher Society of America in that year. This essay restates the individual family/world family metaphor that I have used so often over the years to point to the specific ways we build the larger society through what we do in family settings.

"The Family as a Way Into the Future" was published as a Pendle Hill Pamphlet in 1978. This essay reflects the understanding that has led to my use of the term *familial grouping* to describe inclusively the many living patterns that allow human beings to nurture one another, care for older and younger generations, and ensure that the human race has a future. The essay also reflects my increasingly strong feeling that the family, far from becoming residue on the scrap-heap of history, is in fact both path and vehicle to a better future. There will be pain on the journey, but also joy.

It happens that the essay closes with the same sonnet by Kenneth Boulding that begins this introduction. The "one small plot of heaven" concept has survived decades of the strain and stress of two very unlike people struggling, working, and loving in harness. It has come to full flowering in my mind on this home stretch of family life for Kenneth and me. Our tiny retirement community in Boulder is an extended family in itself, adding to the richness of our six-household, fifteen-grandchildren family spread from coast to coast—all working, each in our own way, for the Peaceable Commonwealth on earth.

Children and Growing Up

Children and Solitude

When William Penn—that extraordinary composite of polished courtier, daring statesman, disciplined seeker, and devout Quaker saint—found himself in a period of enforced retirement through the ill favor of the reigning monarch, he "kissed that Gentle Hand which led him into it," for he found his solitude a great treasure. His little book, *Some Fruits of Solitude*, is the treasure shared. It never fails to lift the spirits of those who are "persuaded to stop, and step a little aside, out of the noisy Crowd and Encumbering Hurry of the World, and Calmly take a Prospect of Things."

Steeped for the past twenty years in the Quaker reverence for solitude and silence (though in the midst of a busy life), I have come to feel it is the most natural thing in the world that children, like adults, should need and cherish times of solitude. The desire to supplement my personal experience and religious convictions about the matter with current thinking from the fields of sociology and psychology led to some revealing hours spent browsing through social science literature on child development.

I found that discovery of the importance of the socialization process in the development of the individual, which gave such a tremendous impetus to the growth of all the social sciences, seems to have completely obliterated awareness of the kind of growth that takes place in the individual when she is *not* interacting with others. The only attention given to aloneness is as a pathological phenomenon, under such headings as introversion, withdrawal, alienation, isolation, or just loneliness. The positive aspects of solitude are ignored. A glance at the card catalog of our university library under the heading of solitude reveals that this is a subject attended to chiefly by poets and German metaphysicians.

The one word that does appear in the sociological literature is privacy, and there is very often an edge of desperation to the word as it is used. Privacy is something defensively longed for, rarely achieved. It has been suggested that the only legitimate place left for privacy in our culture is behind the wheel of a car, and that this is why men and women prefer driving long distances to using public transportation.

We have a real compulsion to groupism. We alternately drive ourselves into groups because we feel it is selfish to stay apart, and bury ourselves in groups because we fear to be alone. A few voices in the wilderness have cried out against this. In the essay "Individualism Reconsidered," David Riesman begged us to develop our private selves, claiming that on this all advances in science and morality depend. William H. Whyte, in *Organization Man*, painted a pitiless picture of men umbilically tied to The Group, The Team, The Organization.

In examining the positive functions of solitude in the development of the individual, child or adult, we are moving against the mainstream of thought of our time. The commitment of behavioral scientists is, in their complex language, to view individuals as vastly complicated receiving and transmitting stations in a finely veined network of such stations embedded in a complex supernetwork society, which is further interwoven into the geophysical structure of the globe to comprise the biosphere. It must be acknowledged that the concept of stimulus-response opened a great door to psychologists in their effort to understand how humans came to comprehend, relate themselves to, and interact with this biosphere. The precision with which physiological psychologists and neurologists have been able to measure the brain's sensory reception of the thousand-faceted stimuli that present themselves at any given instant in time is nothing short of remarkable. Add to this our knowledge about the role various kinds of interpersonal relationships play in the development of the individual, gained from painstaking analysis of interactions in the family, the small group, and the larger institutions of society, and we are faced with an impressive body of knowledge about what makes a child what she is, and an adult what he is. These are not achievements to belittle; they are achievements to be proud of.

But preoccupation with the processes of socialization and adaptation leaves unexplained the Divine Plus in human beings, which renders them incapable, in the long run, of simple adaptation to their environment. While it has been productive scientifically to view humans as socialized animals, this leads to a dead end spiritually if we do not give equal weight to that which goes on inside. I will go further and say that humans *will come to a spiritual dead end* if they do not allow time apart and in solitude for things to happen inside. It is possible to drown children and adults in a constant flow of stimuli, forcing them to spend so much energy responding to the outside world that inward life and the creative imagination which flowers from it become stunted or atrophied. James Nayler, the seventeenth-century Quaker who described his own spiritual journey so movingly in the famous passage beginning "There is a spirit which I feel. . . ," went on to say, "I found it alone, being forsaken." All the saints, God-lovers, and creative spirits through the ages will testify—there are some things that can only be found alone.

Such sentiments are not just a quirk of the religious minded. Our latest information about the interior operations of the nervous system, combined with our knowledge about the conditions of creativity, must lead the hardiest agnostic to insist upon the importance of solitary meditation in the development of the human mind. It used to be thought that all our perceptions of the world around us were images cast upon the blank screen of the retina, and that closed eyes confronted only the blank screen, except for occasional weird flashes of inexplicable color. We now know, however, that there is a continuous ideo-retinal light, sometimes referred to as "luminous dust," which generates a continuous succession of vague shapes and colors "before our eyes," so to speak, although the process takes place inside the retina and inside the brain, whether the eyes are open or closed, whether the person is asleep or awake. There are similar auditory phenomena and quite possibly other continuous sensory stimuli that have not yet been isolated. They are internally generated by normal body processes. The vividness and variety of these inward images and sounds vary enormously from person to person, but the basic phenomenon is universal, like breathing. Normally, our inward images and sounds interact with stimuli from the outside world and we are conscious only of the fused result. One reason why the world never looks exactly the same to different individuals is that this world is always filtered through the physiological light pattern unique to each individual.

What do we make of this? It would be possible to discuss all the visions of the saints as "luminous dust" (was this perhaps what the Lord made Adam out of?), and equally possible to go to the other extreme and close our eyes and ears to the outside world, claiming that these interior experiences are the only true, God-given ones. But this duality—dust of the earth and image of God—is one which the very fact of our creation challenges us to encompass. It is interesting to note that participants in sensory deprivation experiments, such as those in which subjects are placed in a darkened, cushioned compartment arranged in such a way that they can see, hear, or feel nothing outside themselves, cannot endure this condition for more than two or three days. The experience of what might be called continuous hallucination becomes too overwhelming when not counterbalanced by input from the outside world. Such continuous hallucination unchecked by other realities moves rapidly into psychosis.

Our wants for our children are very inconsistent. While we are anxious on the one hand that they fit as smoothly as possible into the social grooves society has prepared, we also want them to be "creative." We in our time set great store by creativity, because we recognize that it is creativity which sets us free from our grooves and enables us to realize all the God-given potentialities within us. We know that it was the tremendous exercise of creativity in the Renaissance and the Age of Enlightenment which produced the explosive and exciting development of twentieth-century society. We also dimly realize that only a tremendous exercise of the creative imagination is going to help us find our way out of the deadly nuclear dilemmas we face in the world community.

Year after year, research piles up on the conditions of creativity, the steps in creative problem solving, the theory of innovation, and so on. And what does all this research tell us? First, that creativity is a fundamental characteristic of the human mind, and that there is no sharp dividing line between the creative thinker or artist and the "ordinary" human being. Unlike the ant, we are incapable of completely instinctive behavior. Everything we do, no matter how trivial, is in some sense an innovation, simply because we never do anything twice in exactly the same way.

Second, the essence of creativity is a recombination of elements, a putting together of things in a slightly different way than they have been put together before. This is as true of a three-year-old's drawing of a tree as it is of Einstein's theory of relativity. Fragments of knowledge and experience have been recombined to create a new synthesis.

Third (and here I vastly oversimplify a large body of data), there has to be *time*. There have to be large chunks of uninterrupted time available for creative activity. We are accustomed to the demand for solitude as a foible of the creative artist or an ascetic craving of the saint, but we have not realized what an indispensable condition it is for all mental and spiritual development. It is in these chunks of time that the great interior machinery of the brain has the opportunity to work (both at the conscious and uncon-

scious levels) with all the impressions from the outside
world. It sorts them out, rearranges them, makes new
patterns; in short, it creates. This is not to say that creative
activity can go on only in periods of undisturbed concen-
tration. Such times may alternate with long periods when
the conscious mind turns to other things, while the unconscious stays busily at work on the sorting and rearranging
process. But the workings of the unconscious are of little
use to us if we do not spend sufficient time organizing
these labors with our conscious mind.

Woe to the one who disturbs conscious creation! Brahms
nearly killed a zealous young man who climbed a ladder
outside his study window in order to watch him at work,
hoping to find the secret of his inspiration. Great were
Brahms' anger and frustration at the intrusion on his solitude, which broke a complex train of mental processes and
rendered him incapable of ever finishing the piece. He
never tried to go back and finish compositions thus interrupted, because the complex silent kaleidoscope of sound,
once shattered, could not be recaptured.

Solitude. Is it not a beautiful word? If we snatch it rudely
from our children, what use can they make of their inner
riches and outward experiences? What use have we made
of ours? H.G. Wells began his *Experiment in Autobiography*
at the age of sixty-six with the despairing cry:

> I need freedom of mind. I want peace for work. I am distressed
> by immediate circumstances. My thoughts and work are encum-
> bered by claims and vexations and I cannot see any hope of release
> from them; any hope of a period of serene and beneficent activity,
> before I am overtaken altogether by infirmity and death.

Since childhood he had dreamed of a Great Good Place
that he would build and work in, and at the end of his life
he said sadly, "Perhaps there is no *there* anywhere to get
to. . . . We never do the work that we imagine to be in
us, we never realize the secret splendor of our intentions."
Wells himself succeeded far better than most in alternating
his attention between the inner and the outer worlds, and

while he never permanently resided in a Great Good Place, he got inside often enough to produce one the most significant intellectual syntheses of the modern era, *The Outline of History*.

What secret splendor of intentions resides in the heart of every child? In most cases we will never know, but from time to time a poet or writer reveals glimpses of the inner world of her own childhood, or parents or friends record their observations of a child who has grown up to make outstanding contributions to the world in adulthood. Walter De la Mare collected such records in a book entitled *Early One Morning In the Spring*, which every parent, teacher, and worker with children ought to dip into from time to time. These children admittedly made unusual use of unusual gifts. But the point has already been made that such gifts are present to some extent in every child. The children described all made special use of solitude. They had opportunity to develop their gifts. They were not being vigorously socialized from morning to night.

The word De la Mare used most frequently to describe the children is "watchers." These youngsters stood slightly aside from the mainstream of life and observed and pondered, "recording experience in the silence of the mind." Isaac Newton was "neglectful of play," a sober, silent, thinking lad, one who was "continually knocking and hammering in his room," making the mechanical models that led his mind to the frontiers of knowledge of his day. Joan of Arc, whose mind was never fed with the written word, began to hear voices as she worked in the fields. Somehow in her solitude, she gained the strength to rise above the conventional expectations of behavior of her time, and "dared to live a life apart in the reality of her own mind"—a reality which encompassed practical political action beyond what the boldest of her fellow countrymen contemplated. Herbert Spencer, the first great English sociologist, was noticed by his father sitting silently by the fire when a very small child. Suddenly the little boy broke into twittering. "On saying, 'Herbert, what are you laughing at,' he said, 'I was thinking how it would have been if there had been nothing beside myself.'" This little philosopher grew up to carry wads of cotton wool in his waistcoat pocket for use when involuntarily exposed to dull conversation! Lord Herbert of Cherbury—poet, philosopher, soldier—declared his parents thought him stupid because he could not learn to speak, but that actually he refrained from speaking because he felt there was nothing important to say. Imagine the astonishment of his governess when this silent sage one day opened his little mouth and asked, "How came I into this world?"

The Quaker psychologists Victor and Mildred Goertzel pointed out in *Cradles of Eminence*, a study of the childhoods of famous persons who lived into the twentieth century, that a childhood period of "time out" was important for the maturing of the creative powers of these men and women. The time out might have come as a result of illness, of family crisis, or a move to an isolated place. Whatever the cause, a drastic break in the usual routine which left these children thrown on their own devices for a lengthy period of time was remembered in later years as having special significance for their inward development.

The Goertzels cited Einstein, who when he was fifteen found school so intolerable that a school doctor finally gave him a "certificate saying he had a nervous breakdown and must spend at least six months with his parents in Italy. . . . He wandered through churches and hiked through the Apennines. It was at this time that he began to ponder what would happen if a ray of light were to be imprisoned." At the age of sixty-seven, Einstein himself wrote, "This delicate little plant [the holy curiosity of enquiry] aside from stimulation, stands mostly in the need of freedom; without this it goes to wrack and ruin without fail."

Well before the time when a child can consciously make use of time alone, however, comes that critically important moment in a life which represents the dawning of self-consciousness. All later intellectual and spiritual development depends on this emerging sense of identity. "I stood one afternoon, a very young child, at the house door, when all at once that inward consciousness, *I am a Me*, came like a flash of lightning from heaven, and has remained ever since." This was Jean Paul Richter's experience. It may not happen in early childhood. It may not come until adolescence. But many of us if we look back introspectively can recall some special moment of realization. In spite of its momentary character, the memory stays on. Gerald Bullett makes the indelibility of this experience very vivid:

> I came upon a four-year-old child standing alone in a sunlit country lane . . . the summer sky arching over him. . . . The moment . . . has nothing at all of drama or poignancy . . . nor could I hope to express in words . . . the meaning it holds for me. But if I shut my eyes and hold myself very still, I no longer see that child: I *am* that child. The chalky road is hard under my feet and brilliant to my eyes; I feel the sun on my hands and face, and the warm air on my shins. . . . Except for this aloneness, this sense of *me*, it is perhaps a purely animal or sensual experience, and it occupies, as I conjecture, the merest point in time, a fraction of a second.

Why is such a moment so important? And why is aloneness an essential part of it? I am not sure that I know the answer, but it may be because this is the first conscious integration of the world outside with the interior world of the young mind. In the act of conscious integration, which is a heaven's breadth away from simple unquestioning acceptance of the world of sight and sound, a sudden mastery is gained over the interior machinery which sifts, sorts, and combines what comes in with what is already there. It is the first great step in spiritual development, because it involves recognition of Creator and created. The subduing of the will, the proper discipline of the mind, and the spiritual understanding of the *me's* true place in the universe all come much later. Solitude is essential because this is an experience of separating out from the world in order to integrate with it. It cannot happen if the mind is distracted by constant social stimulation.

Along with this release of the sense of identity, which is growing gradually all the time and is not necessarily marked by the sudden expansion of understanding described above, there is also a continually expanding awareness of spiritual reality. I believe this awareness is present in all children from a very young age, but it takes different forms depending on the kind of environment and teaching a child receives. Obviously, some children are better at articulating it than others. Because awareness of spiritual reality depends on experiencing the invisible as real and present, it is likely to flower most in children who have times alone.

Göte Klingberg of Sweden did a study of the religious experiences of children between the ages of nine and fourteen, and the most meaningful experiences these children recorded did not often take place in church settings, but occurred when they were alone in the house or the woods and fields. It is not surprising that sometimes a child is dealing with fear of aloneness when he or she comes to a religious experience. One boy described an October evening when he was left at home alone to look after a sleeping little brother. He tried to bolster his courage by thinking about God. Suddenly, he felt that God was *there*, around him, in him, as he sat by his brother's bed. A twelve-year-old girl described a long walk home from a friend's house in the late afternoon. It was growing dark, and the path lay through a gloomy wood. "I imagined that God walked by my side and that I said: Dear God, take care of me on the way. And I imagined that God answered: 'See I am with you.' Then I felt very calm as I went along."

Fear of being alone, when met by a child who has had a sensitive upbringing by understanding parents, often becomes the means of developing an awareness of spiritual reality. In the memoir *Quaker Childhood*, Helen Thomas Flexner wrote of her childish fear of Satan, who lurked in dark and empty rooms and closets in their commodious home:

> At nighttime Satan grew very bold. The whole house was haunted by his presence. Every empty room, even my mother's, was full of him, so that when I was forced to go upstairs after dark on some errand I begged my mother to send her voice with me. While the magic refrain, 'I am here! I am here!' sounded in my ears, however faint and distant up the long stairway, I was not afraid. •

To rely on the reassuring voice in the threatening darkness was as big a step for that child as for the anguished adult to rely on the still inward voice in the emotional darks of maturer years.

There are many kinds of aloneness, and they are by no means all desirable. Feelings of isolation and abandonment do not necessarily lead to experiences of God's presence. The children here described came from homes and church communities in which loving and careful nurture had already given them a store of experience to draw upon in time of need. The more I study the religious life of children, the more I recognize the importance of providing a child's mind with materials to work with. The roles of parent, teacher, and minister are crucial indeed. So are the books a child reads—and how quickly we recognize the imprint of the Scriptures on the expressions of a child who has been wisely steeped in them!

Unfortunately, recent generations of parents have developed a very negative attitude toward steeping the mind of the child in Scripture and the language of religious experience. We have seen the unfortunate results in past generations of children who have emerged from such upbringings mouthing meaningless stereotypes and expressing a false emotionalism. A child left alone with a Bible in our time is more apt to evoke horror than admiration. A child all alone is bad enough, but put that black book in his hand and you are really asking for trouble!

It is true that many children of the past labored under a heavy burden of doleful religious imagery and admonitions. We feel a pang of sympathy for the little Quaker girl reflected in Jane Pearson's journal, written at the turn of the nineteenth century:

> It pleased the Lord by his good Spirit, to work in my heart in my young years: which brought goodly worry over me, and fear lest I should be taken away in my childish follies. When the bell used to toll for those of other persuasions, oh! the awe and inward fear attendant on these occasions! I would say in my heart, these are now called off the stage of this world, and fixed as for ever they must be.

We also long to comfort young William Dewsbury, who "delighted in lightness and vanity . . . [and lived] without fear of God," and then suddenly heard the word of the Lord at the age of eight: "I created thee for my glory; and account thou must give me for all thy words and actions done in the body." William spent the years until he was thirteen tending his sheep and seeking an acquaintance with the God of his life, a lengthy stretch of solitary anguish for a preadolescent.

This, however, is not the whole story by any means. In the close, warm communities of these early Friends meetings (where, wrote Thomas Clarkson in his *Portraiture of Quakerism*, domestic bliss was the chief recreation and source of enjoyment), children knew life, love, and fun as well as the somber truth of the Time of Reckoning. In the long stretches of solitude open to the young of that less cluttered age, they worked out their own solutions to the conflicting inward and outward pulls they felt. Living in "colonies of heaven" in a sea of revolution and violence, they made their own observations and developed their own ideas about what the Lord required of them. The more outgoing they were, the more they responded to the outside world. This made their inner conflict more intense, and the resolution more colorful. These resolutions did not come in ready-made scriptural formulas, or through the application of external admonitions, although the latter were certainly not wanting. Scripture and admonitions were but among the many seeds sown in the heart, and each child brought forth his or her own individual fruit. Ruth Follows, an eighteenth-century Friend, wrote of the loving upbringing by precept and example she had, and the struggle that ensued after the death of her mother in early adolescence:

> I left her counsel behind me, trod her testimony under my feet and took a large swing into vanity, frequenting such company as had like to have proved my utter ruin. But blessed be the Lord! He closely followed me with his sharp reproofs, and . . . stopped me in the midst of my career, and took off my chariot wheels, so that I could not overthrow nor yet keep the pure Seed in bondage.

Benjamin Bangs, a first-generation English Quaker, wrote lovingly of the seeds of wise religious instruction sowed by his widowed mother, and of the pulls that his fun-loving nature exerted on his more sober intentions.

> When I was between eleven and twelve years of age, I was much given to divert myself in running, wrestling and foot-ball playing, which was much practiced in the part of the country where I lived, and my company was very much desired by such. . . . Being one day by myself, not far from the place of our habitation, I met with such a visitation, as I had been altogether ignorant of before, in which a sweet calmness spread over my mind; and it rose in my heart, that if I could but keep to this, what might I grow up to in time? It much affected me, and rested with me for some time.

John Woolman recorded in his journal the first conscious memory, at age seven, of his lifelong capacity to integrate images of spiritual and physical reality:

> As I went from school one Seventh Day, I remember, while my companions went to play by the way, I went forward out of sight; and sitting down, I read the twenty-second chapter of the Revelations: "He showed me a river of water, clear as crystal, proceeding out of the throne of God and of the Lamb, etc." And in reading it my mind was drawn to seek after that pure habitation which I then believed God had prepared for his servants. The place where I sat and the sweetness that attended my mind remain fresh in my memory.

Sarah Stephenson, of that first generation of children to come under the influence of the inspired early Publishers of Truth, wrote of the time before she met the Quaker ladies who were to change her life that she was torn between a "natural disposition" to vanity (her father being a rich merchant), and what was surely an equally "natural" inclination to love the Lord, and to seek to be alone with him while still a child. The seemingly trivial words of the Quaker elder Elizabeth Ashbridge, "addressed to me in the language of unspeakable love, 'what a pity that child should have a ribbon on her head!'" were enough to set her permanently on the Lord's path, ribbonless.

What is the significance of these records, chosen out of hundreds of childhood recollections by Quaker journal-keepers of past centuries? Quaker journals contain enduring evidence that the child's spirit is the most fertile ground in the world, and that seeds planted unnoticed bring forth unanticipated flowers. Ruth Follows, Benjamin Bangs, and John Woolman each had the guidance of a deeply spiritual mother and the storehouse of the Bible to feed their young minds; experience of the "world" served only to stimulate the growth of that which was early prepared inside them. Sarah Stephenson had only stray crumbs of spiritual instruction, yet was able to build deep meaning out of what she had. As one reads these journals, one finds again and again the same incredible richness and variety of human experience in the encounter with the Creator that we find recorded in the Bible. Is there any better summing up of the complexities of the adolescent encounter with God than "the Lord took off my chariot wheels"? Knowledge of Scriptures has never cramped a child's spirit; the cramping comes only through the lifeless rendition of Scriptures by uncomprehending adults.

If the crisis of identity is the crisis of the twentieth century, then we must look well to this aspect of the nurture of the twentieth-century child. We are standing on the threshold of the cosmos, and we do not know who we are. Either we discover our identity and move into a new dimension of spiritual existence along with our technical conquests of time and space, or we shrink back into sub-existence as a race of well-trained clerical assistants, timidly feeding data into gigantic computers to find out what to do next. Who is taking "time out" to probe for new dimensions that will open up a way of life not now imagined? Who is dreaming dreams? Who is seeing visions? Where are the solitary ones?

They are all about, but they are too few, and we make it very hard for them. Are icy mountain peaks their only natural habitat? No, for solitude can be full of joy; it can vibrate with life and warmth. Rather than bereft and isolated, we may in times of solitude be more deeply in tune with Creation than human contact alone could ever permit. The person who has felt that sense of glad at-homeness in the universe knows solitude's deepest joy. The child in times of aloneness is no stranger to such happiness. A ten-year-old boy in Göte Klingberg's group writes, "Another time I was up on the hill near my house. I went there and was looking at the flowers, and then I thought, 'So beautiful. Has God really done this?' And I felt so happy."

Have we not each of us inadvertently stumbled on a child's solitary joy? Our eldest son used to come home very late from his weekly guitar lessons, and not until several years later did I learn that he would sit down in a wooded field on the way home and play to its invisible inhabitants. Then I understood in retrospect the look of serenity on his face when he returned home after those trips. His younger brother, then aged eleven, brought me these lines after I explained to him what I was trying to write about:

> It happened when we were playing in the little woods. For some reason I lay down while everyone else ran off and played. As I lay down on my stomach with my hands holding my cheeks, I watched the wind blow gently through the trees. Oh the silence of nature was beautiful even though the wind was blowing and the birds singing and the leaves crackling. Even though there were these noises, they were still soft and quiet.
>
> The way the high grass was so yellow and leaves so green and the sky so blue with its swift clouds. It seemed as if I was with God in Mother Nature's palace.

Each of us has our own recollections of solitary childhood joy, hidden away deep in our minds for safekeeping. When I look back, I can find a small girl all alone in a rowboat in the middle of a quiet mountain lake at high noon. Scarcely big enough to handle the oars, she sits alone feeling the warmth of the sun, the cool blueness of the water lapping softly at the boat, and the immensity of the fir-covered hills all around. She is bursting with warmth and bigness and silence. This is home. It is belonging. It is joy.

These, then, are the fruits of solitude for children: a sense of who and what they are, whence they came, their place in God's world. And out of this positive and secure relationship with the universe comes the freedom to "play" with creation in the best sense of the word. The things they see and hear can tumble around inside their finely tuned minds, interweaving with their inward store of knowledge to produce further creation. The products need not be mathematical formulas, complex social insights, or symphonies or paintings or poems. The beautifully ordered life, sensitively lived, its daily tasks performed for the love of God, represents one of the highest forms of integration any person can achieve, and if it were not so, we would not still sit at the feet of Brother Lawrence, the humble and illiterate monastery dish washer. His insight that "our sanctification consists not in changing our works but in doing that for God's sake which formerly we did for our own" represents as creative an interior integration of knowledge about the world as Newton's insights on gravity.

How do we adults help make creative solitude available to our children? First, surely, by finding meaning in it for ourselves. Solitude has many faces: reflection, creation, prayer, contemplation, mystical union with the All-One. "Delight to step home, within yourselves," said William Penn. Forbidden fruit for busy parents and exhausted social activists? Rather the bread of life. And adults who seek it do not need to explain it to children. Children have an instinctive understanding of a withdrawal by adults into solitude, as memoirs often testify. Helen Thomas Flexner recalled that she was told her grandfather spent an hour every morning and evening listening to God.

> So when I came suddenly upon my grandfather one day seated motionless in his armchair with closed eyes I knew he was not asleep. He was talking with God. I stopped short where I was and stood very still. Perhaps if I listened intently enough I might hear God's voice speaking to my grandfather. But the room remained quiet, not even the faintest whisper reached my ears. After a long time my grandfather opened his eyes, saw me, and

smiled at me gently. These moments of intense listening for God's voice in the room with my grandfather are among the most vivid memories of my early childhood.

In homes where silence is lived, the child finds it easy and comfortable to turn to it. In a large and noisy family (like my own) the period of hush that begins every meal sweeps like a healing wind over all the crosscurrents that have built up in the previous hours, and leaves the household clean and sweet. Times apart of special family worship, hard to come by in the daily routine, become hours to be remembered and valued for their very scarcity, and never fail to catch us up to another level of love and awareness. In these times we rediscover who and what we really are, as individuals and as a family, and can lay before God what we cannot easily lay before one another. It is an odd thing to say, but solitude can be shared. In a family where inward solitude is highly prized, individuals may slip easily into and out of each other's solitude. Some families must work harder than others to create the physical situation in which times of solitude become possible, but when silence is treasured, the quiet place is found.

The silence of the Quaker meeting for worship opens a unique door into solitude for the child who is fortunate enough to experience this corporate listening. Rufus Jones wrote in his wonderful record of his Quaker boyhood, *Finding the Trail of Life:*

> It does not seem necessary to explain Quaker silence to children . . . they feel what it means. They do not know how to use very long periods of hush, but there is something in short, living, throbbing times of silence which finds the child's submerged life and steers it to nobler living and holier aspiration. I doubt if there is any method of worship which works with a subtler power or which brings into operation in the interior life a more effective moral and spiritual culture. Sometimes a real spiritual wave would sweep over the meeting in these silent hushes, which made me feel very solemn and which carried me—careless boy though I was—down into something which was deeper than my own thoughts.

I cannot resist adding a passage which describes a presumably typical late nineteenth-century meeting for worship attended in childhood by William Fryer Harvey, recorded in *We Were Seven*. (These were two-hour meetings, by the way.) It is very revealing of the natural interplay between the sense of religious awe and the love of fun in the child's mind, and should set us at rest about the child's capacity to handle solemn experiences. Little William has been squirming through the first long hour of silence, and has just now listened uncomprehendingly to a message delivered with deep conviction by an older Friend whose face is lined with suffering:

> I feel that he is a good man, that what he has said has not been lightly spoken. For some minutes I am conscious of a feeling of awe. Then the ticking of the clock claims my attention. I become aware that the cracks in the plaster of the wall are extraordinarily like the map of Norway and Sweden. Charlie [his brother] gives a great sigh and drops his handkerchief. Then we all rise to our feet and Charlie climbs on to his footstool as grandmamma offers prayer. She is the only one in the meeting who wears the old-fashioned Quaker dress and bonnet. She is like a beautiful dove. Her face shines with an inner radiance. When she has finished we sit very still. The hand of the clock moves very slowly. Suddenly a strange fancy seizes me: what would be the best way of arranging the Friends in meeting in a series of fights? How would they be most evenly matched? William Stout and Samuel J. Hay, M.A. were about the same height, and though Samuel J. Hay, M.A. was much heavier, I thought and hoped that William Stout was the more active. The two elder Miss Thistlethwaites would be evenly matched, but who could best take on the young and energetic Miss Thistlethwaite? Kate? Mrs. Turnball? or Mrs. Howgate, the caretaker's wife? The hand of the clock is moving very quickly now. Almost before I realize, it is ten minutes to twelve and grandmamma is shaking hands with John Henry Probyn. Meeting has broken up.

A lot can happen in a boy's mind in two hours!

Whether they are awe-struck or mischievous, we know in our hearts that our children must have solitude in order to do the kind of inward growing we cannot plan for them. Are we not then required to reflect on what is happening to our own lives and the lives of our children? Each year that passes cuts more deeply into the precious silent hours our souls require. What is happening to our children as a result of the fact that their time is so heavily scheduled both in and out of school, and even increasingly in summertime—that once golden time of inner ripening for the child?

The chancellor of one of our major universities made the alarming comment some years ago that the greatest danger of our time is "unoccupied minds," and that the best way to counteract it would be to have students go to school all year around. Time is our greatest resource, said this educator, and no moment must be wasted. The year-round calendar leads to the fully occupied minds that ensure our coming out on top in the bitter struggle for national survival. Might it not rather be that *unoccupied* time is the only thing that can lead to the creatively occupied mind? I certainly share the concern for right use of time, but suggest that an Inward Scheduler may be a better guide than an outward scheduler in determining that right use. How can outward schedules allow for the really important claims on the mind? Amy Lowell used to drop ideas for poems into the back of her mind, as into a letter box, and let them incubate. Then at the right moment (announced only by the Inward Scheduler) she would drop everything else to "attend to the arriving poem." Any obstetrician's secretary knows that births cannot be scheduled by the desk appointment calendar!

Dare we leave spaces of time free for the promptings of the Inward Scheduler? Dare we have faith in the workings of the spirit-illumined intellect? Walter De la Mare says of the child's mind: "There is a natural instinct to preen the wings and choose the food and water; as will a goldfinch in its solitary waste, converting into song and beauty and energy the seed of a thistle." Can we believe this?

The Personhood of Children
and the Flight from Relationship

What I have to say about relationship comes out of a year of solitude. Solitariness makes relationship very precious. A new sense of self evolves in the hermit's cell because in aloneness a person can spread invisible wings, send out crumpled-up antennae, open all the eyes in the body, attune the inward as well as the outward ear. While it is in part a centering self, it is also very much a reaching self that emerges. At the same time that concern with the self fades away, a marvelous attunement with the individual other develops. Going to the grocery store after some days alone, the plain face of the grocery clerk comes alive with hidden glory. Each person one meets becomes infinitely precious.

This is hard to sustain in the midst of people. Their preciousness soon fades under the pressure of the demands they make, unless one keeps looking at them with the inward eye, hearing them with the inward ear. Mostly we cannot bear to be fully present to too many people. It exhausts us.

There is a reason for this flight from relationship, guiltily compensated for by the establishment of encounter groups, extended families, and the many devices we have dreamed up to make us listen to one another against our own inward volition. We are the first humans to live with such high densities of population, of communication, and of artifacts. The population explosion and its accompanying technological explosion have created a new condition for humankind. We are not well adapted to the change. The ways in which we have tried to adapt have been partly good, partly bad. Our lack of success shows up mainly in the high levels of violence both on the world scene and within our own country. Many things have to be worked out before we can deal adequately with that violence, including learning how to share the fruits of the earth with everyone in the earth-family.

For Quakers and others who have with George Fox smelled the new Creation, world-changing activities must grow out of a realization of the divine-human society. The divine-human society involves human relationships open to the winds of God. Yet everywhere around us we see people sealing themselves off from each other and from God. This is one way of dealing with unbearable human density, and unbearable rates of change.

Child-adult relationships have suffered particularly from the sealing-off process, which is expressed in the phenomenon of age grading. Age grading throughout life—not just temporarily in one particular stage such as the teenage years—is one of the most pervasive features of modern urban society. Even the Society of Friends has not done enough to overcome it within its own community.

Age grading means that toddlers are kept with toddlers, kindergartners with kindergartners, elementary, secondary, and college students with their own, young married couples and young parents with their own, middle years and retired and golden-age folk with their own. We move right through life in lock-step fashion with our own age group.

"Why do teachers hate children?" This half-angry, half-bewildered question shot right into the middle of a First-Day school class I was teaching. My response was immediately defensive. I was being stereotyped as a public school teacher forever riding herd on children, when in fact I was a college professor who liked being with kids and did this for fun. "I am not a teacher!" I wanted to say—to escape the stereotype. Then the thought came to me: could my young challenger say, "I am not a child"? And I was

overwhelmed by a sudden awareness of the heavy stereotyping we lay on children, by how trapped they are in the
stereotype of their own childhood. Adults can move into
many roles: they can be parents, spouses, breadwinners.
They can participate in a whole set of special communities—religious, service, civic action, and recreational. In
each of these roles the adult is treated as an individual with
special characteristics relevant to that role, but a child is a
child in every setting. Children can never break out of the
oversimplified expectations of their behavior. They can
never expect attentiveness to their special capacities unless
they are programmed into an adult-created situation.

Age grading has consequences far beyond blocking
people's ability to appreciate individuals of all ages. It
contributes directly to the generalized levels of social violence in a society, by fostering a condition that social scientists call *social autism*. The term autism ordinarily refers to a
pathological condition in which an individual's absorption
in need satisfaction or wish-fulfilling fantasy serves as a
mechanism of escape from reality. When social groups
insulate themselves from each other, images of social reality are distorted. Substantive communication between
groups lessens, producing an escalation of distrust (the
less we know what others are doing, the more certain we
are that they are doing something bad); and there is a
general inclination to blame "them" for everything that
goes wrong. The phenomenon of social autism almost
guarantees that children will have a difficult time assuming
cooperative roles when they themselves become young
adults. The anthropologist Ruth Benedict pointed this out
years ago, contrasting the situation of children in many
tribal societies, who interact freely with adults from earliest
childhood and do not go through the "adolescent rebellion" we think is a built-in feature of growing up.

Another consequence of age grading is the absence of
opportunity for members of each age group to be challenged by the social perceptions of other groups. All age
groups live in an atmosphere of unreal sameness of social
view, and can evade the confrontation with inconsisten-

cies in their own thinking that is a precondition for moral and spiritual growth.

There is also a failure to develop common perceptions of responsibility across the age gaps. When high school and college students of Boulder, Colorado seized a bridge on the main artery between Boulder and Denver as a protest against the mining of Haiphong Harbor in 1972, stopping all traffic for nearly twenty-four hours, they felt they were acting in a socially responsible way. They were letting their fellow citizens know that business could not go on as usual, that people must stop and think, reassess their priorities, effect a change in foreign policy. Yet the word the furious citizens of Boulder and Denver used most during the period was "irresponsible."

The effect of age grading is compounded by the fact that children do most of their interacting with adults other than parents and teachers in front of a TV screen.

Finally, age grading unnaturally loads the child-parent relationship—the parent becomes the adult world for the child. We all know what a trauma moving and changing schools can be for a child. Some researchers on depression have found that significant changes in life situation can create depression for individuals of any age. Such changes always involve some disruption of social relationships. A study of five thousand patients coming to a certain psychological clinic over a period of years indicated they had all experienced disruptions in relationship prior to the onset of depression.

What makes people so vulnerable to debilitating depressions when the inevitable disruptions of relationship come? In part, it is the breaking apart of that cozy, homogeneous age-grading group that insulates one from the larger reality. Until the insulation can be reconstructed in a new setting, the individual often feels helpless. People who have developed their sense of identity and security in multi-aged groups, who are adept at moving back and forth between a variety of social settings, do not experience this terrible social nakedness when their life situations change.

Developing a variety of child-adult relationships is not a panacea. It won't cure everything that ails us. But these relationships provide a very rich resource for dealing with the world, and for acquiring the kind of interactive skills that make us confident, competent, and helpful in a variety of life situations. The child-parent relationship cannot bear all those burdens.

Our children do not, on the whole, live in a very nurturing society, despite all our claims to the contrary. They do not feel respected by adults. Respect for the child is found more often in tribal societies than industrial ones, perhaps because tribal societies depend more on their children for the welfare of the group. Every pair of hands is needed, from the age of four or five on. Not all tribal societies are nurturing to children, any more than all parents in industrial societies are aggressive and demanding. But we do have an instructive example of different attitudes toward children right here in the United States. Some American Anglos are becoming aware of the horror many native Americans feel for the lack of respect shown by Anglos for their children. Native Americans are becoming increasingly articulate about their own values—including non-violence—in familial and community relationships, and their need to prevent the erosion of these values by Anglo influences.

The saddest aspect of the naked ape myth is that it is reinforced by stereotyping and isolating the child. Stereotyping is twice cursed: it shrinks the character, perceptiveness and social creativity of the stereotyper, and it stunts the growth of the stereotyped. It unleashes hostile, insecure young adults on a society that is already fearful. We don't *have* to play the age-grading, child-stereotyping game, but we do. Instead of finding new ways to bring our children into partnerships with us, we exert endless ingenuity in developing programs for them.

But what *are* we to do? We don't know what to say to each other, across the ages. We don't know what to do together. Even the extended-family projects of Friends meetings and other churches, designed for people who are without families or who feel isolated in their own, often tend to plan most activities without children present, so adults can be "relaxed" and engage in "grown-up" talk. Adults who work hard during the day feel they have a right to be free of children for their recreation.

Furthermore, there is a very real asymmetry in child-adult relationships. As Kenneth Boulding puts it, the adult can remember being a child, but the child cannot remember being an adult. The adult has an experience bank to draw on that the child and young person do not. She can evaluate persons and events in the light of situations encountered in the past. To pretend that young people "know as much as we do" when in fact they don't is hypocrisy, and does not provide a basis for mutual respect. To recognize the contribution they have to make is *not* hypocrisy. Fresh energy, enthusiasm, and imagination are distinct resources—and they complement the resource of experienced judgment. In fact, neither is much use without the other.

No matter how we adjust to the asymmetry, however, it is there. The gap between youth and age is a wide one, and not easily crossed. Part of the trouble lies in the fact that we give little conscious attention to child-adult relationships outside the child-parent relationship. Whenever we start focusing on the generation gap, we always revert to looking at children as children-in-families, thus putting the emphasis on parent-child relationships. Women have just freed themselves from always being treated as wives and mothers. Why cannot children also be freed from always being treated as sons and daughters? There is a good reason why children, right through the college years, don't like to participate in the same gatherings with their families. They are not treated as individuals, but only as the son or daughter of the X's.

We need the concept of an "open family," comparable to the concept of open marriage which created so much interest when a book by that title was published several years ago. In an open marriage, husband and wife carry on activities and friendships independent of each other, as well as together. What open marriage really means is that wives now have as much social autonomy as husbands have always had. In an open family, children would carry on activities and friendships with adults, independent of their parents. *The crying need in our world is for child-adult friendships outside the family.* This would relieve the senselessly overburdened child-parent relationship. Teachers and Scout leaders provide some relief to parents, but from the child's point of view that means simply being shifted from one parent-authority figure to another. Children need adult friendships to prepare them for creative social roles.

Martin Buber's "I-Thou" relationship sprang into my mind as I was groping for a way to describe what the child-adult relationship could be in a more peaceable, less rigid society than our own. What is the I-thou relationship? There are many ways to describe it. I think of it as listening to God in another person. It is simply being fully and totally there to a person, with all five physical senses, and tuned in with the sixth sense, too.

We have had Quakers in our midst who possessed this gift for treating every child as a Thou, and they should be remembered and celebrated as models and teachers for the rest of us. I am thinking particularly of William Bacon Evans, who will live for many years to come in the memory of every child who was ever enchanted by the specially designed treasure store he always carried around in his pockets.

There is a poignant story called *How the Children Stopped the Wars,* based on the children's crusade of the 1100s, in which a young shepherd boy, Uillame, conceives the idea that if all the fathers who were away fighting could *see* their children and *know* their presence, they would stop fighting. After many adventures and hardships, the tired, ragged children find the battlefield, having added the children of the enemy to their numbers enroute. They step uncertainly into the midst of the battle. The soldiers stop, astonished. In the lull, Uillame feels he ought to say something:

"Sirs!" he said. "We have arrived from very far away, to see for ourselves what it is you are doing here. Back at your homes, land is growing dry, the orchards have gone, your houses are falling to ruin or are burnt. We want to see the victory you are achieving here. Don't you remember us? Don't you remember who we are?" . . . That was all he could say to stop them; simply to show them they were there. . . .

The soldiers on both sides were infinitely tired, and they had begun to feel that the wars might last forever. . . .

Suddenly one of them shouted, "That's my son!" . . .

Which side had been fighting which was forgotten and each man tried to find the child who was related to him. . . .

That night they slept together—huddled like grown bears and bear cubs, the fathers, the sons, and the daughters, among the ruins of that broken battleground.

By morning the fathers were ashamed to remain at this place any longer. They couldn't fight, with their children looking on.

The story is a fable, not a strategy for stopping wars, but there is a profoundly important insight here about the role of the child in society, and about what happens to adults who insulate themselves from children. First, the children bring a different perspective to the battlefield. *We want to see the victory you are achieving here.* Second, they are being present to their fathers as listening, loving human beings. As long as the fathers could insulate themselves from the social reality they were presumably fighting on behalf of, they could go on with military destruction. Once the children invaded that reality as a living presence, the rationale for the destruction broke down.

Age grading insulates us from the living realities and enables us to manipulate people as objects, to treat resources as pawns in a chess game. Children are certainly objects of concern both in the larger society and in the Society of Friends. That is the problem. They are *objects* of concern, not *subjects*, and it is in the nature of our perception of objects that they are to be manipulated (Buber's "I-it" relationship). Children are manipulated by being left alone and given meaningless freedom to make non-choices about how to spend time. In the name of allowing them independence and freedom, the adult is absolved from

responsibility for what the child does and the child is manipulated into thinking that she ought to feel free when
she may really feel lonely and bored. It is a great device
for making children feel guilty. Children are also manipulated by over-programming their time in the name of making the best opportunities available to them. Programming
parents may drive their children all over town but never
really interact with them. Either way, the adult does not
need to spend time being *present* to the child.

The plainest way to describe the life of a child is that
she is moved from programmed space to programmed
space, and each space has an authority figure posted over
it who has absolute rights over her in that situation. Since
Quaker parents do not normally inflict serious abuse on
their children, or subject them to harsh behavioral constraints, they may not see the lack of rights for children
as serious. Many children do receive serious abuse, however, and the subtler exercise of authority disguised under
the "make your own choice" rhetoric doesn't fool children
who realize perfectly well what they are expected to do.
The same situation obtains in schools, including some of
those most dedicated to "developing the child's potential."
The young man who asked why teachers hate children did
not come from an authoritarian school.

Our passionate commitment to the development of individual ability and the individual personality puts us in a
ridiculous situation. We are faced with a revolution of
rising expectations among the young, and think bitterly
back to how docile and obedient we were in our youth. If
only we had been tougher with these kids, many are saying, all would be well now. And what are children saying?
Adults don't respect us. They don't treat us as persons.
They never listen to us. Whenever I talk to children and
young people about the problem of relating to adults, I
always get the same answers. Children perceive that adults
don't want them around.

Yet how exciting it is to be with children when they feel
at home and treated as equals. At the Ghost Ranch, New
Mexico gathering which resulted in the founding of Inter-

mountain Yearly Meeting, two high-school boys joined the discussion group on "Nurturing the Spiritual Life of Our Children." It had been agreed in advance that the participation of young people in any discussion group would be encouraged, and these two young men took the program committee at its word. There was a distinct uneasiness in the group as they sat down with us. What were they doing there, in a discussion on spiritual life and particularly the spiritual life of children? It turned out that they were very concerned about spiritual life, their own and that of adults. They had thought a lot about it. They had more to say than a number of adults present. And they had advice for adults on how to relate to the spiritual life of children: "Listen to them. Find out what is going on." We adults fumbled for a way to relate to these boys who were being so frank and open with us. Respect for children was talked about. The boys brought up equality. What does equality for children mean, the adults wondered. No problem for the boys. Equality meant being recognized as equally human, equally aware, equally searching. Not equally knowledgeable—not in everything, anyway. But it turned out there were some things these boys knew that we didn't know. It often doesn't occur to us how interested children are in the things we do. When did you last invite a twelve-year-old to a dinner party just to participate in the conversation?

Some meetings develop a custom of many child-adult friendships. Community life in such meetings becomes rich, as does the spiritual life, and the spoken ministry in meeting for worship. Through all the postwar years of demonstrations, vigils, and fasts, children and young people in many meetings were side by side with adults in every action, through the worst weather and the most hostile public receptions. In Ann Arbor it was the teenagers who made the connection between violence in Selma and violence in Vietnam. They declared a three-day fast and wore signs saying "I'm hungry for peace in Selma and Vietnam." Elementary-school children joined them. Finally the adults joined, too. Mothers complained that they could not eat when their children were fasting!

We should not be surprised when children and young people take leadership. It is an old Quaker tradition, and many tell their children the story of the children of Reading Meeting, who continued to meet for worship while their parents were in jail. A number of early ministers of the Society of Friends were teenagers, some as young as thirteen and fourteen. In the eighteenth century, working-class children would have been in the labor force from the age of ten, and would be very accustomed to being among adults. Children had a hard life in those days, but among Quakers, at least, they also had respect.

We need a closer partnership with children today because we need fresh perspective on our activities. We need their insights, and not only in the arena of social action. We need their spiritual insights, too. In thirty years, I have never taught a First-Day school class without receiving new teachings myself. One of the great lessons of my life came many years ago when I was discussing prayer with a class of five-year-olds. We talked about all the different ways you could talk to God, and when we had (I thought) completed a list of kinds of prayers, Peter Blood burst out, "There's the gladly prayer, too!" There is indeed a gladly prayer, something different from prayers of praise and prayers of thanks. I never had a word for that kind of prayer until Peter gave it to me.

The basis of serious partnership with children is recognition of common interests. That discussion on prayer with the five-year-olds did not come out of the blue. I had already discovered that young children had their own experiences of inward listening and prayer, through their own spontaneous comments and through my reading of childhood recollections in Quaker journals and other autobiographies. The problem was to find a way to talk about these experiences—one that would strengthen the children's own inner growth and not reduce the understanding they had already gained to conventional religious language that would infringe on the spontaneity of the original experience. Since all children love stories about Indian life, a study of Native Americans led very naturally to an exploration of the Indian ways of prayer, fasting, and seeking visions. From there it was but a step to their own prayer life.

The children from meeting communities that encourage a lot of child-adult interactions are the ones, I suspect, who become the most creative and active young adults. Much of the life of the Movement for a New Society came out of that kind of interaction, and it continues through the very nature of the Life Center communities with their age-spanning memberships. Many of the young people in these communities had the experience of being listened to and respected when they were children. They developed a sense that their thoughts and actions would make a difference. Probably in the childhood of every activist peacemaker there were one or many experiences of being trusted and attended to by an adult. Such experiences build up a reservoir of competence and inner security which makes it possible to take risks on behalf of what one believes.

Quakers are committed to risk taking. That, I think, is what the Society of Friends is about. We can become better risk takers by trusting children.

The tradition of child-adult partnerships can die out in a meeting or other church community if it is not continuously fostered. Such partnerships develop naturally when there are a number of families with children the same age who do many things together. In such situations all the adults and children come to know one another well, and there is little age grading. If a church community does not have a fortuitous combination of highly congenial families with children, can it develop child-adult friendships? Yes, but not without some attention to the process.

Having meeting gatherings which bring people of all ages together for play is one of the easier ways to build child-adult friendships. In Boulder one May, we danced around a Maypole (most of us for the first time in our lives). In December we danced around an outdoor Christmas tree which we had first decorated with popcorn, birdseed, and suet for the birds. One-to-one relationships are the hardest to establish, because people feel awkward and shy. There are many in-between approaches, such as bringing every adult individually as a visitor to the First-Day school. Everyone in a meeting community can be included in a teacher-apprentice program. People over the age of eight (and younger too!) have something they can teach others. Everyone should take the responsibility to sign up for the program and learn a new skill or interest, thereby building friendships. This takes time and thought, and a lot of bolstering of nervous adults.

Inviting children and teenagers to monthly meeting to speak about their concerns, and then taking time to develop joint projects with them on the basis of their concerns, is one valuable way to *practice* respect for the young and develop meaningful partnerships with them. In all child-adult relationships, there must be plenty of room for adult listening.

Does the adult world have time for all this? Is the broadening of opportunities for child-adult relationships really so important? Isn't it more effective to specialize? Wouldn't it be more satisfactory if we concentrated on being the best possible parents we know how to be, seeing to it that for the rest of the time our children are with the best possible teachers and youth leaders? Yes, if we can be satisfied with the kind of society described in George Orwell's *1984*, in which all problems are solved by technological programming, and all utopias are private. If we want to rediscover human joy and wholeness and creativity, and if we want to learn to care for our planetary household as one earth-family, we cannot continue to insulate adults and children from each other. Children need to be present to us—and we to them—"on the battlefield," so we will understand what kind of victory we are achieving.

Born Remembering

Not in entire forgetfulness,
And not in utter nakedness.

But trailing clouds of glory do we come
From God, who is our home.

- Wordsworth, "Intimations of Immortality"

Everyone has had some experience of early childhood remembering: remembering an otherness not to be explained by family experiences, stories heard, events witnessed. Why is it that we are born remembering, and live forgetting? Is this a joke that God would share with us, but that we can only laugh at in the moment when we have come full circle, and remember again? That coming full circle and remembering again is no laughing matter, however. It is a conversion experience, literally, and life cannot go on as before. This happened to me, and I am going to spend these pages reflecting on the remembering, and the forgetting, and the remembering, as I have experienced them in my own life.

There are cues for remembering in my own early childhood. I grew up in a tiny immigrant Scandinavian community in a small factory town outside Newark, New Jersey. Everyone had come over from the old country to seek a better life—in part for themselves, but most especially for their children. It was a kindly community and we had many festive occasions together in the group of a dozen families or so that had relatives spread out over northern

New Jersey, Long Island, and Brooklyn. Thinking back over the many feast days we shared together, and especially the holy days of Christmas and Easter, I am suddenly struck by the fact that no one in our community ever went to church. We knew of a Lutheran church where evening services were held in Norwegian, but no one ever went. We all knew it was good that the church was there, and every home had a Bible in it. I have a distinct memory of someone's aged great-grandmother in a lace cap sitting quietly reading the Bible when the rest of us were being jolly. But religion was never discussed.

For all the jollity of our time together—and I used to love going to those parties right up to my early teen years—there was nevertheless an underlying air of anxiety in that community. This was in the 1920s and early 1930s. Did everyone have a job? The best possible job? Were promotions coming? Were the men "succeeding"? Were the children doing well in school? One family knew some mysterious important people in New York. Could they be gotten to put in a word in the right place for a hardworking father or a promising child? Sometimes yes, sometimes no. So while we all had lots of affection, a lot was expected of us too. And I, along with all the other children of those families, had to justify the emigration by my life performance. This was the process that I continued working out until the fiftieth year of my life.

In my own family, besides the expectations, there was also an unseen Presence. That is how I know I was born remembering. My mother and father never talked about God, never used petitionary prayer, and only read the Bible once a year, on Christmas Eve. Yet God was present. Father had been given the great old Norwegian family Bible when he was a young man. He was the youngest son in a large family and by rights the eldest should have had this Bible. But grandfather always felt that my father had a religious calling.

As a child, father had been even more somber than I. If he indeed had a call, he resisted it in the sense that he never trained for or practiced a religious vocation. Shy, he became an engineer and poured out his love for God and his wife and children in the ways that shy people can: through a thousand affectionate deeds. And on Christmas Eve the family Bible came to the supper table, and father read the Christmas story from Luke by candlelight. He almost sang the words, he loved them so. Afterwards we lighted the tree (my earliest memories are of real candles) and joined hands to dance around it. First we walked sedately and sang the Norwegian carols about the babe who lived in his Parent's house in heaven but came down to us on this evening long ago. The dancing songs that came later were fun, but I always loved the carols about the babe best.

What led me so often to sit quietly in my room listening to God when I was little? To struggle with reading the English Bible (the Norwegian was too hard for me) back from Luke to Genesis, and forward to Revelation? Listening to God is one of my clearest childhood memories. There was always a quiet inner space I could go into, a listening place. I listened while picking blueberries in a sweet-smelling meadow; while lying in the bottom of a rowboat rocking on the ripples of a small mountain lake; while curled up on the living room couch leafing through the reproductions of Norwegian paintings that were among the few treasures brought from our home in Norway.

I wasn't listening for voices. Yet the sense of God's presence was often with me. What could it be but remembering? It became so strong that by the time I was nine I found a church with a Sunday school so I could study more about the Bible. I do not know how I came to choose the church I did. It was some distance away—perhaps two miles. I walked back and forth alone, and never missed a Sunday. The pastor's wife taught a high-school class which I used to think about wistfully. I loved my own class, but the teacher didn't know what to do with my questions. After a year or two—certainly long before I was in high school—the pastor's wife took me aside one day and asked if I would like to come into her class.

God bless Mrs. Northwood! She sensed that here was someone longing to learn what she was longing to teach! In her class we never worked with anything but the Bible itself. How those hours flew! Sometimes she would invite me to her home after school, and read Henry Van Dyke aloud to me in her living room. Reverend Northwood and his wife were both pastors in the truest sense of the word. They had a calling to make God's presence real for others. I don't recall that Reverend Northwood had any special oratorical gifts, but his sermons always held me completely because I felt he *knew* God. To this day, going into any church and sitting down in a pew fills me with an unreasoning sense of joyful anticipation. Another legacy from that time is the fact that I have found ways to continue year after year to teach Sunday School, even after our own children have all left home. I love to share with children what was shared with me when I was a child.

The fact that I have been able in some way to reach back to the early rememberings, to the freshness of the feeling of God's presence as I knew it when small, has been enormously important in keeping what wholeness there has been in my life. The inner listening place I developed so early has always been there for me in a very conscious way during times of unbearable stress. It is a space that cannot be crowded. And yet, as an adult, I lost the feeling of the immanence of God's presence. I only remembered the space.

All children are listeners, but some stop listening and remembering sooner than others. When our own children came, I was very conscious of their need for listening when they were small. When I realized that many parents feared their children might be abnormal if they spent too much time alone, I studied accounts of children's listening in Quaker and other autobiographies, and wrote an essay about children and solitude (included in this book).

It makes me sad when I hear discussions about not introducing children to "God" until they are old enough to understand. I *grew* into the Lord's prayer, and I am still growing into it. All religious language, all devotional books, and particularly the Bible, provide growing room for young minds and spirits. They have sometimes been used as straitjackets by adults who did not understand, but this does not mean that they *are* straitjackets.

While I knew Jesus the babe who came down from God's house to be with us, the other Jesus—the elder brother, the teacher, the Lord—did not become a part of my life until those Sunday-school years a little later. I came to understand that while God is present across an unmeasurable farawayness, Jesus is present with the nearness of a friend; while God teaches through being, Jesus teaches through speaking and doing. But these understandings did not come smoothly. Giving Jesus his "right" place has never been easy for me, perhaps because I loved God first. Was it perhaps a little bit like the experience of the only child having to make room for a sibling? Nonsense, of course, because Jesus is in the first place the elder brother, and furthermore he is not a displacer but a way-shower. Still, the struggle has been there.

Since I needed a teacher, I came to love him as a teacher. A little later I went through the "Jesus as boyfriend" stage. During several summers spent in the environment of lusty religious enthusiasm at Ocean Grove on the New Jersey shore, I discovered this unexpected dimension of Jesus when I was otherwise boyfriendless. That way of relating to Jesus did not last long, because it did violence to the Otherness which religion invoked for me.

Many years later, very unexpectedly, I came to experience Jesus in an inward way as a teaching Presence. I had been going through a spiritually dry period and at a small Quaker gathering was engaged in one of those verbal harangues on spiritual matters that we often use to cover our own emptiness. Suddenly he was there, silent and intent, and I heard and saw my babbling self. Quieting down quickly, I felt taught without words. He stayed with me for some days after that, and returns from time to time, though not often. He does not come in time of crisis, but in times of spiritual barrenness.

When did I discover Mary? I am not sure how old I was,

but standing one day before her statue in a small village Catholic church, I felt her presence. There has never been any ambivalence in my feelings about Mary. Mother, sister, holy lady, she was with me through all the turbulent high-school days, through all the vicissitudes of my atheistic period during college—and she has stayed with me ever since. I prayed to her countless times during the early years of our marriage when it seemed as if we would never have children. When the babies started coming, she was close to me through each of the five pregnancies. Though I am sure the children would be astonished to hear me say it, she helped me raise them. In dark times, I find a Catholic church and kneel before Mary. While intellectually I know that I don't need a statue to kneel before, I accept my childlike spirituality when I need her strength.

My last year in high school was full of the turbulence of the insecure achieving adolescent. There was no money to send me to college; my two younger sisters born ten and twelve years after me, and whom I loved and mothered, would need the modest family resources even to see them through high school. Yet the whole migration to America had been so my generation could go to college—an achievement unthinkable for our status and income group in Norway. With his whole soul my father wanted his three daughters to go to college! The day I won a scholarship that would cover almost the total cost of tuition, room and board for four years was a great day for our family. It also meant a new addition to a familiar burden—I would now have to redouble my efforts to justify that original migration, by also justifying the scholarship through my college years. Fearing weakness, I suddenly saw my love of God as a sign of weakness. My religion was a crutch, and I must learn to walk alone, to be strong.

The college application form which routinely asked my religious faith produced a torrential denial of religious belief, covering pages which were appended to the application form. To me the whole world seemed to hang on what I said, though this lengthy document had no place in college routines and probably went into the wastebasket as unfileable!

My stiff, intellectually impeccable deportment through college with regard to things religious was occasionally modified by visits to what seemed to me intellectually respectable places like the Christian Science church and the Quaker meeting. Since religion had been so central for me since earliest childhood, life was too bleak with *nothing*.

The Quakers unexpectedly touched me—"spoke to my condition," in the straightforward words of George Fox. Not very deeply at first, because I was wearing a heavy armor of rationalism which nothing could get through. The silence of the meeting was a reminder of my own childhood listening place, however, and there was no gain-saying my at-homeness there.

The first year out of college, when I went to New York to conquer the world and found myself first running a billing machine in one publishing house and then rewriting impossible high-school textbooks in another, was the first major time of reckoning for me. Did success and justification lie in this crowded, noisy, competitive city?

I worked hard at my jobs because I was trained to do that. I also participated in a kind of office party life which left me feeling confused and out of touch with reality. It was a value world I had had no previous experience with. But in between the parties the Lord led me to some lovely places. A freckle-faced young man at the editorial desk next to mine was a devout Catholic and ardent pacifist, and spent his free time working with a Catholic hospitality house in Harlem run by a woman I knew only as the Baroness. Now while religion had not been verbally articulated very much in my home, pacifism had. My mother must have been one of the most ardent pacifists of her generation, although circumstances placed her in settings where she never connected with peace movements of any kind. During my high school years in the mid-1930s she was pouring out plays, essays, and poems on pacifism while the early war clouds gathered in Europe. So my office friend spoke a language I understood, though I had never encountered peace movements either in high school or college.

The day he took me to visit the Baroness's storefront center was a real turning point for me. To find in that sordid city (New York seemed very sordid to me though I also loved it) a place where people very frankly and openly loved God and fiercely worked with and on behalf of Negroes was like being lost in the dark and suddenly finding home—though the home was so different from anything I had known that I could not be totally at ease there. I had lived among ethnics all my life, both North and South European, but never among blacks.

The Baroness—Catherine de Hueck—was a Russian émigré who ruled the little Harlem center with all the grandeur of one accustomed to walk with czars and princes, but she was also a person with great purity of heart. Later she started a remarkable spiritual-cum-social action community in Canada. This lady of rank made a profound impression on me. She was not the least bit interested in being a "success" in America. She lived in poverty, and wore that poverty like court jewels. She was as brave and independent a person as I had ever seen, yet was not afraid to be on her knees in prayer. With a critical mind that cut like a knife through fuzzy thinking, she nevertheless saw all social reality as at core a spiritual reality. The defenses I had acquired so painfully in my college years were useless here.

Another lovely place the Lord led me to was John Haynes Holmes's church (the town hall on Sunday mornings). Here I heard one of the great pacifist preachers of my youth, and again saw a person of stature frankly loving God with all his heart, and using his intellect in ways I did not dare use mine.

I heard of Dorothy Day, editor of *The Catholic Worker*, but never met her. Having carried an image of her in my heart ever since that long-ago time in New York, I was delighted beyond belief to find, when I finally met her in 1974, that she was as young in spirit as I was still imagining her in years. Thirty years in time were erased!

The impact that these persons made on my life was out of all proportion to my contact with them. I did not stay in New York more than five months in all. The contrast between the moral stature of the Baroness and Holmes and my own life was too great. I realized that I was in the wrong place. I almost lost my inner listening space because I could not cope with the city. One day it became absolutely clear to me that I could not cope. What turned out to be a very minor stomach upset and skin rash had announced itself to me as the voice of doom, and I literally fled the city.

Based briefly with my family again, I started modestly back to school, having found my way to a small graduate-student stipend. The campus seemed a safe haven for my battered soul. Instinctively I sought out the Friends meeting, but I also found a Catholic church with a statue of Mary I could visit. Mary's presence and the Quaker silence together got me anchored. Shortly afterwards I met Kenneth Boulding at a Quaker meeting for worship. The signals were so clear to both of us (and apparently to the entire Quaker community of upstate New York) that we were to share our lives, that we announced our intentions of marriage only seventeen days after we met.

While in one way I had been preparing for the world Kenneth Boulding introduced me to all my life, in another way this was a new world to me. It was the Baroness and John Haynes Holmes, Quaker version. Kenneth's own deep spirituality released the last of my own inhibitions about the religious dimension. He was himself going through a period of great religious stress at that time, suffering because his family back in England was enduring the bombing raids from Germany while he was sitting safe in America. His intellectual analysis of the futility of war and his religious commitment to peace combined to produce, during the course of that year we met, the first in a long series of books that were to lay the foundation for the peace research movement, and the collection of poems that has become a much-loved spiritual classic, *There is a Spirit: The Nayler Sonnets*. He was as gifted in the ministry then as he is now, and when he spoke in meeting the tears often rolled down my cheeks in love and joy and compassion for this extraordinary man who was to be my husband.

We read aloud a lot to each other in those days, and Brother Lawrence's *The Practice of the Presence of God* prepared me best for the years ahead:

> That in the winter, seeing a tree stripped of its leaves, and considering that within a little time the leaves would be renewed, and after that the flowers and fruit appear, he received a high view of the providence and power of God, which has never since been effaced from his soul. That this view had perfectly set him loose from the world, and kindled in him such a love for God that he could not tell whether it had increased during the more than forty years he had lived since.

My own heart was so full when I read this that I felt I could never love God more than I did at that moment. And when the occasional twinge came, about whether I really should marry just then, or whether I should go overseas and do the reconstruction work I was in training for during our "courting summer," Brother Lawrence again spoke:

> That our sanctification did not depend upon changing our works, but in doing that for God's sake which we commonly do for our own.

Kenneth and I took the founding of our little Quaker "colony of heaven," as he later described marriage in his "Sonnet for a Quaker Wedding," both seriously and joyfully. We did indeed endeavor to make our home a center of tranquility and peace, that all who entered might find refreshment therein, according to the old Quaker advice. It was always a community center, and when the children came it was a children's center too. Because we had waited so long for them to come, each of the children seemed a very special blessing. I used to stand over their cribs and pray at night when they were asleep. By day we endeavored to keep a Quakerly peace, though with turbulent boys it was not always easy.

These were for the most part happy years, and I found myself often thanking God in the midst of mundane tasks like changing a messy diaper. It seemed to me that in those tasks God's love shone most clearly. This was the meaning of incarnation. I used to keep the words of Brother Lawrence, John Woolman, and others who particularly spoke to me on cards above the kitchen stove. During the times I felt this overflowing love, I wanted to sit down and write some of my prayers and reflections to share with other mothers. I knew that all were not as happy as I. And knowing how hard my own somber times were, I wanted to share when the joy was there. I truly regret that I did not, but it was almost a physical impossibility during the years when I was spiritually the most ready to do it. The daily round with five small children is such that there are few moments a mother can take in quiet.When our fifth child was born we really were a *large* family! A Quaker meeting, like a Catholic parish, is a fine place to bring children up when families do many things together—worship, play, and share the ups and downs of life. There was a group of about six families in our meeting which shared so much that in a sense we all raised each other's children. To this day we are one huge extended family, traveling any distance to be together for special life events like the next generation's marriages. We were all equally active in the peace movement and in local community projects. While we were also concerned with the nurture of the inward life in our families and meeting, the community action often got in the way. I was not the only young mother in the community who had a need to justify her existence! There was, I believe, undue busyness. God was never absent, but often ignored, and I did a lot of forgetting in those years, especially as the children grew older.

Thus it came about that at the age of fifty-one I confronted a conversion experience. All the changes associated with the lessening intensity of family responsibility led to the realization in a blinding flash that I had "lived forgetting."

A conversion experience is never as sudden as it seems. It is always preceded by a period of mounting inner tension. For me the immediately preceding years had involved returning to the university for a Ph.D. in sociology, moving from the community in the Midwest where the children had grown up to a town nestled at the foot of the Rocky Mountains, and trading the emptying nest at home for a professorship at the university. From rearing children to teaching college students, from community action to research on the dynamics of peacemaking, from the up-and-down spiritual life of one Quaker meeting to the up-and-down spiritual life of another Quaker meeting—where was all this going?

In spite of the sense of an unnamed catastrophe occasioned by the United States' continuing presence in Vietnam, activities went on much as usual in the suburban middle-class world I lived in. We tidied and cleaned our much too roomy and overfurnished houses, cooked unnecessary quantities of food, moved in our daily round quite protected from suffering of every kind except the peculiar dull aches of affluence.

"Part I" of my upside-down turning, and the beginning of another remembering, came in India in January of 1971. After chairing a congress of the Women's International League for Peace and Freedom, I gratefully accepted the invitation of the director of the Gandhi Museum to stay with him and his hospitable wife. In the very modest unheated apartment of my friends, who chose voluntarily to live at a level of simplicity considerably more austere than that of most Indians of their class, I discovered the human condition through the very ordinary experience of being terribly cold day after day! It was January, temperatures went below freezing every night, and each morning I would read in the paper about the number of Indians who had frozen to death in the streets the night before. What a small amount of extra food, clothing, shelter, and warmth would have kept them alive! I drew my own coat tightly about me in the evenings as the damp fog rolled into the apartment from the river, and thought of all the extra shelter and warmth spread in wanton abundance across Suburbia, U.S.A.

All the usual distances between me and physical deprivation were erased. A school was to be built at the top of the hill to one side of the house in which I was living. Three migrant construction worker families lived there in brush shelters. I saw the meager bowls of rice that were cooked for the evening meal. In the morning I saw the men swing mattocks into the steep hillside to loosen stones which the women, babies on their backs, carried up the hill on their heads to crush for building materials. Small children of unguessable ages climbed up the hill with smaller stones, occasionally stopping to play. The men sometimes sang, the women and children sometimes smiled. For a few days I lived a triple life: part of me was back in our suburban home in Colorado; part of me was shivering in my friends' apartment; and part of me was next door living in a brush shelter and cooking meager rations over an open fire.

By day I sat in the Gandhi library absorbing the writings that had poured from Gandhi's pen during his life. As I read his passionate words about *sarvodaya* (welfare)—not wanting what the least of his brothers and sisters could not have—I knew that these were my brothers and sisters too, and that I also could not want what they could not have. I wrote long letters home about stripping ourselves of what we did not need.

Readiness for stripping—or shall I say a "call" to strip—is a very individual and personal thing, however. Coming home to my family, I found that words could convey neither outward experience nor inward state to Kenneth and most of the children. The two children who were already called to this were finding their own ways of expressing it. For the rest it was simply unreal.

And so I lived in suburbia again. All around me were well-intentioned, socially conscious people, supporting good causes. At Friends meeting on Sunday mornings I would sit in the silence with all these good people, listen to words of kindly mutual encouragement and often poetic insight, and return as they did to the domestic comforts which sealed us all off from the living God.

Part II of the remembering involved in my conversion occurred a few months later when a teenager badly damaged by drug trips and going through a major emotional crisis came briefly to stay with us. He had been one of the flower children, one of the gentlest of them. Conscious of nothing but his desire to give and receive love and to hurt no one, he was in deepest inward agony.

Watching his suffering, knowing that in a certain way I was as trapped and helpless as he, I suddenly saw myself one night as a small frog in the bottom of a deep well, leaping and leaping to get up and over the side. All my life I had been leaping. I knew where the sun was, I knew which way to jump, I knew there *was* an outside—another place to be. Yet I kept falling back into the bottom of the well.

We have all heard that a drowning person sees her life unreeling past the inward eye in her final moments. In just that manner, and in just a few moments of time, my own life unreeled before me. This was a kind of death—the death of that old try-hard frog, the birth of a new creature who found her way over the top of the well and into a new world. In that moment of leaping, I felt as if I were living not only my own past life through, but that of all people who had ever lived—all my brothers and sisters on the planet. I saw how we all chained ourselves to daily rhythms which were bound to defeat us. Day after day we recapitulated the old cycle of effort, irritation, impatience, and anger—softened by small epiphanies of love and remorse. The spirit had to break through from time to time, because spirit is our very nature, but how tiny the eruptions, how heavy-handed our daily behavior. For how many millennia had this gone on? Was the human race never to discover its self-forged chains?

The snapping of my chains signaled for me that the human race was indeed to be freed—in theological language—from the bondage of sin and death. My experience was one of the simplest and oldest religious experiences that come to humans, no less transforming for its commonness. Was the leap an act of the will or an invasion of grace? At such times, grace informs our will. God does not carry us as so much baggage. The tension of the preceding years uncoiled like a giant spring in the crouched figure at the bottom of the well. It was met by God's grace, and I sprang up, free.

Knowing I was a "newborn," I felt I must learn to do everything anew. The shell of the old me was still there, and represented a real danger. I had fifty-one years' worth of old habits, trained responses, ways of thinking and doing that could pull me back into the well. I tried to pray continuously, and to metaphorically put my hand in God's, so that I would not walk "on my own." Over and over as I walked about the campus and carried on my work I would whisper prayer phrases like:

> God, be in my feet and in my walking.
> God, be in my hands and in my touching.
> God, be in my eyes and in my seeing.
> God, be in my ears and in my hearing.
> God, be in my mind and in my thinking.
> God, be in my heart and in my loving.

I tried not to do anything I could not put God into, in that way.

It is hard to teach when you are a newborn! It is not a time for lecturing. I did the best I could, and tried to share other dimensions of the teaching-learning process than the cognitive. Fasting for five days shortly after I came up out of the well helped me stay centered. It made me a bit physically shaky as I carried out my rather heavy daily routine, but that was part of the newbornness.

Early morning rising and prayer before the household stirred also helped me stay centered. Needing the love and support of those around me who could not relate to what was happening kept me humble, and grateful for the love that can hold a family together even in the absence of full understanding. I shared what was happening with Kenneth. He had gone through his major spiritual upheaval long ago, and felt at peace. But he never failed to let me know that he was standing by. Increased sensitivity to others who were in an intense state of seeking brought new fellowships in unexpected places.

At times, I felt both very distant from and very close to the Society of Friends—distant from the Friends immediately around me with whom I could find no way to share my experience, but very close to the "Quaker saints" who had been part of my religious formation in the early years of my life in the Society. I was keenly aware that both Fox and Woolman had come through experiences like mine, and found much support in that.

The historical "communion of saints" became very real to me as I found help in many quarters. First came Joachim de Fiore, whose concept of the new Age of the Holy Spirit (described in Marjorie Reeves' *The Influence of Prophecy in the Later Middle Ages*) started my thinking about the very possibility of a new human condition. Then there were two writers who gave me a most vivid understanding of the incredible process of *remaking, reforming* the human material: Evelyn Underhill and, oddly, the anthropologist Victor Turner. The way in which Underhill patiently traced out the lineaments of the mystical experience in her masterful work entitled *Mysticism,* and analyzed the disciplines that went into the tearing apart and reforming of those touched in this way by God, made the unbelievable believable. Turner, who wrote *The Ritual Process: Structure and Antistructure* in a totally different context, described the function of *liminality* as a rendering of the ordinary social being into prima materia which can then be molded anew. This is the function of the ritual process, which was the focus of his study. Again, the unbelievable became believable.

The saints themselves (though Evelyn Underhill was surely a saint too) helped in other ways, by writing of their own experiences. I felt that my own love of God was shallow compared with Teresa of Avila and St. John of the Cross. And as I read *The Heretics,* Walter Nigg's book on saints, heretics, and warriors for God, and explored the writings of the God-intoxicated women and men of the Middle Ages, I found a very different set of role models than those sociologists usually write about. I realized that at one point in the Middle Ages it really had seemed as if the Age of the Holy Spirit were dawning. The intellectual and spiritual energy unleashed by that perception makes the spiritual explorations of the twentieth century seem tame by comparison. But something went wrong. It petered out in famines, plagues, crusades, and witch hunts.

The petering out preyed on my mind. Social Darwinism and the easy optimism of the age of science at the dawn of our century seemed to me to be equally out of touch with the grimness of history and with the underlying evolutionary possibilities of humanity. Teilhard de Chardin (whose work I had long loved but only now understood) was the one prophet of our age who saw, like Joachim, through the grimness and to the coming divinization of the world. The possibility of rebirth was still a live possibility for the human race. How, then, was the petering out to be prevented?

It seemed to be my task to explore that question, and I did not know how to go about it. What did God now require of me? I had not been brought up out of the well for nothing. Was I to lay aside the still-new role of college teacher and live a life of prayer? Since it seemed as though most of the people around me simply weren't serious about life, did not recognize that they walked on holy ground, breathed the breath of God, and moved toward a far-off divine end, I feared that I too could not remain serious if I went on doing the things I had been doing. I questioned particularly the use of the intellect. Was it not precisely the constructs of the human intellect that so effectively shut us out from the experience of God's immanence in the created world?

For one whole summer I sat before my desk, work spread out before me, and cried. God gave me no ease. There was no "There, there, it will be all right." It wasn't all right, and I had to struggle through. Meister Eckhardt's austere teaching comforted me. The directed will was my responsibility. This I understood. How grace could work on my directed will I did not understand. "Why don't you let

God be God in you?" asked Meister Eckhardt. If only I could!

It was only at the end of that summer that I came to the gradual comprehension that God is always at work in us, even though there are times when we are too numbed by pain to realize it. The gradual lessening of the paralyzing conflict that made me unable to work, and also unable to find ease through prayer, was certainly helped by the reading of Jean LeClercq's *Love and Learning and the Desire for God*. Once I realized that monks also had to face conflicts between scholarship and prayer, that choosing a "life of prayer" did not avoid that conflict since the church too had need of scholarship, I got some perspective on my struggle. The intellect was also part of God's creation and could, like anything else, be used or misused.

By fall I had a certain feeling of resignation about the difficulty of the path before me. In spite of a loving family and loving friends, however, the aloneness was hard to bear. One of the ways I had tried earlier to deal with my concern about our excessive affluence was to try to interest congenial people in a type of community living which would involve sharing things in common to reduce individual possessions and expenditures. Such a community was, of course, to involve more than simple living. It was to affirm a different conception of humanness, and of society. Many communities have been founded with similar intentions in recent years, including one directly related to my own efforts. There is certainly a social readiness for this.

The old question of individual readiness, however, became once more a barrier. Just as my own need for community was lessening through my learning to let God be God in me, I most unexpectedly found a community of the spirit which allowed other ideas of community to recede to the back of my mind. Friends at the Newman Center found a small Benedictine monastery at Cold Spring on the Hudson that was willing to receive a woman guest for two days.

I had never been in a monastery, and only occasionally

had attended Mass, though always with great spiritual benefit. The words of the Mass and the silence of the Quaker meeting had always seemed to me to point to the same deep place. After a long day's conferencing in New York City, I boarded the Poughkeepsie local with an excitement I did not myself understand. As the train bumped its way along the Hudson River at dusk, I kept repeating, "Here I am, Lord. Here I am!" Brother Victor and a postulant, Brother Patrick, were waiting for me at the station. To my joyful eye they were two radiant archangels. They had waited with vespers till my coming. In the candlelit chapel in the farmhouse monastery on a cold October evening I sang vespers with the brothers, following music and words totally unfamiliar to me, yet carried on wings of prayer to a full participation in the songs of evening praise.

I can find no words to express what it meant to be plunged from the austere silence of the Quaker meeting with its abstention from all outward signs and symbols into the exultant joy of Catholic liturgical celebration. The frog that had jumped out of the well had been sitting pretty forlornly nearby ever since, wondering what to do with new life in a new place. No longer! A great flood of love was released by the singing of the liturgy, and renewal surged through my being.

"Too late have I known thee, beauty ever old and ever new, too late have I loved thee," sang St. Augustine. But not too late. Never too late!

For me the rhythm of monastic life was the long-sought, long-lost rhythm of my own deepest inner spaces. I loved the predawn matins, the quiet hour on my knees before lauds, the going downstairs to a simple breakfast of coffee and a slice of bread after a three-hour vigil of waiting, listening, singing, praying. I loved the quiet reading time in the morning, feasting on books from the monastery library; noon prayers in the chapel; readings from *The Art of Prayer* during lunch; chores, walking, and more reading in the afternoon. What an incredible grace the rule of silence is! Vespers, spiritual conversation during and after supper, compline, and then a long time on my knees alone

in the dark chapel in utter thankfulness for the leading
that brought me here.

During one such prayer time in the chapel, I meditated
for a long time on the cross before me; Christ's outline
could but dimly be seen by the one flickering candle in the
room. I entered into my journal that night:

> Jesus, I am one of your kind! You are what we are to become.
> Yet that sense of kind comes with a sharp sense of infinite
> distance, infinite unworthiness. I, scarcely a speck of dust in the
> world you illuminate. I of *your* kind?
> Unbearable stretching of spirit—torn upwards, rooted below.
> Was that your crucifixion?

When the brothers took me back to the station two days
later, Brother Victor gave me a copy of the singing version
of the Psalms used in his chapel, with a weekly rotation
of psalms written out for lauds and vespers, and the pattern
for compline. I have used them ever since. I needed a
frame to grow on, and this met my need.

I have been back to Our Lady of the Resurrection Monastery many times since that October weekend. There is a
small community of us who gather there: two sisters of
other orders who love the contemplative life, the brothers,
and myself. We are all pacifists, and some of us have been
very active in the peace movement. Our spiritual bond is
very strong and we *feel* like a community, even though we
will never live physically in the same community.

The love of God is an extraordinary bond in today's
world. While my relationship to the little Benedictine
monastery is a very special one, I have also come to find
community with the very tender Catholics, including a
Franciscan sister who works particularly with the student
community at the university; with some of the Sisters of
Loretto, whose life of service of love affirms the reality that
so much around me denies; and with the brothers of the
Christ in the Desert Monastery, who live a life of radiance
in the harsh beauty of the desert.

It is in the very nature of this bond of love to want to

include others in it. Since I couldn't carry my family and my meeting community into this experience of fellowship in the Catholic community, I longed to bridge the gap between the monastery and the home—and I found a way. Brother Victor happens to be an especially fine cook, owing to years of kitchen duty in the very poor monastery in Avila, Spain where he took his vows. He learned there to make tasty meals out of unpromising scraps. One day when we were all sitting in the monastery kitchen preparing the evening meal I suddenly burst out (violating the silence, I fear!), "We should write down all Brother Victor's recipes and make a cookbook. Call it 'From a Monastery Kitchen.'"

Of course, *From a Monastery Kitchen* was intended to be, and is, much more than a cookbook. In working it out we have all thought a great deal about what of monastic life can be shared in families. Each of us has written our own understandings of that sharing. We chose as the theme of the cookbook the Christian Year of Grace. For me it has provided opportunity for much reflection on the meaning of seasons, cycles, and celebrations in relation to our personal lives, the life of the church, and the life of the secular society. There is so much food for the nurture of our spiritual lives in the seasons of the church year, and yet the outer garments of celebration when taken over by the secular society prevent recognition of the underlying spiritual reality. The experiences of advent and birth, of penitence, of death and rebirth, and the great explosion of pentecostal joy, are closed to many Christians, and closed indeed to those who live entirely outside any church. How can the experience be reawakened without contributing to an artificial reconstruction of past customs that leaves out the living core?

In my own religious tradition of Quakerism, the fear of participating in artificial reconstructions led to a witness against all sacraments and all celebrations. We were to live every moment as a sacramental moment, every day as a celebration. What has happened, of course, is that we have lost the sense of the sacramental and have forgotten how to celebrate. Yet this Quaker testimony points to a real problem. The inward cycles of our souls do not correspond to the great cycles of the church. When the church rejoices we may be personally sad, and when the church wears the garments of penitence we may be bursting with inward joy. Learning to let the personal and the public cycles nourish and complement each other is a crucial part of growing up. There is much learning for children and adults alike in the study and celebration of the feasts of the church in the light of variable human conditions. Children who learn about these things in their religious community are lucky indeed.

It has seemed to me a very special affirmation of my continuing sense of community, both with the Quaker and the Catholic faith, to work on a book for families at this time of my life—the empty nest years; the more so because my own calling has increasingly been toward solitude. During my summer of intense spiritual struggle I began to plan, with the help of a young seeker friend, what was to be a hermitage—a place of retreat. We built a simple one-room cabin in the woods up behind our family cabin in the Rocky Mountain foothills not far from Boulder, Colorado. Since we had to carry all building materials up the hill through the woods, this could never have been without the help of my young friend and his builder brother. It was constructed with a great deal of love, because they entered fully into the spirit of what the cabin was to represent.

So gently, so slowly was I led toward thee, Lord! How could I know what that cabin was to mean?

The hermitage was ready on Thanksgiving Day. I came up that weekend to the first solitude I had ever known in my life. I was fearful. I could not imagine what it would be like to be alone, having been surrounded by people all my life, and having needed to be needed all my life. It was very soon after my first visit to Our Lady of the Resurrection Monastery, and I carried the Hours of Office with me.

I am sitting in the hermitage now, writing by the setting sun. It has a window wall framing the mountains, and a tiny prayer closet at the back. It was an intuition of my young friend that even a one-room cabin should have a special place of retirement for prayer. There is electric light and heat, but no water. I go down the hill to the stream for water, and to the privy for a bathroom. I sleep on the floor, cook on a hot plate.

The very first day that I climbed the steps and entered here alone, uncertainty fell away and joy rushed in. On my knees in prayer, a lifetime of longing was being fulfilled. I was no longer the frog uncertainly perched at the brink of the well, or even the grateful frog warbling away in the monastery chapel. I was me, Elise, God's child, at home. In the intervening year and a half, I have never entered this hermitage without being reached out to as I open the door. The hill from the road is a steep one. It seems as if every tree and bush and stone on the way reach out to help me in my climbing. I feel lifted. And when here, I feel enfolded in grace. God greets me here.

My initial rhythm of spending two days a week here was rudely interrupted by ear surgery which disturbed my balance canals and left me wildly gyrating in space for a few days. What an extraordinary experience to have no fixed points of reference in the outside world! On being wheeled into surgery I had sung, "Into thy hand, O Lord, I commend my spirit," and the Lord did indeed hold me when nothing or no one else could.

Catholic Communion was brought me at my request by that good shepherd of souls for many decades at St. Thomas Aquinas Chapel in Boulder who had also become my good friend and spiritual guide. This was a great act of love and faith on his part, since I was not a professed Catholic. Having felt the Presence so totally in the Eucharist at the monastery, I felt the need very acutely in this crisis for the anchoring in Christ which Communion gives.

Each of the very few times I have partaken of Catholic Communion stands out brightly in my memory as a time of meeting, of union, of outpouring of grace. In the St. Thomas Aquinas Chapel in Boulder, in the monastery chapel up the Hudson, in the beautiful sandstone-and-glass chapel at the Christ in the Desert Monastery in New Mexico (where Christ himself might be, if he were living again among us in human form), in the chapel of the Sisters of Loretto in the rolling hills of Kentucky, I have known the joy of oneness with all creation. The spiritual life of non-communing churches sometimes seems arid by contrast. Here is the height of incarnational awareness within the bonds of human fellowship. How can it but transform the lame and limping social institutions we create out of our own frenetic activity?

After experiencing Communion in this transforming way I expected to be inwardly called to profess Catholicism. But God confounds our expectations, and I have learned that my obedience consists in remaining a Quaker. I was sad when I realized this meant that I should no longer partake of Communion, except within the spiritual community I am closest to. How comforting then to read in John Tauler's *Spiritual Conferences*, that there are those who receive "not sacramentally but only spiritually, good people, pure in heart, who long for the Blessed Sacrament but cannot go to Communion at that time. These latter, in the measure of their desire and good dispositions, may even receive the grace of Communion more than those who receive sacramentally." I certainly do not covet *more* grace than those who receive the Sacrament, but I am glad God does not leave me out.

The whole matter of my continuing relationship with the Society of Friends, and of my right responsibilities professionally and in the community, came into focus in a very beautiful way through my reading, just before my hospitalization, of Adolphe Tanquerey's *The Spiritual Life*, the old guide to spiritual training for monastics. Tanquerey writes a good deal about the duties of state. Given one's situation in life, the responsibilities one has already accepted, and the talents one has, there are certain things one must do and other things one may not be able to do. My duties of state include my family, the human community, the Society of Friends, peace research, and students. That sets up a fair number of constraints!

Lying in the hospital I knew that if I was ever able to function well enough to climb to the hermitage again, I would need a year of reflection and retreat to work through all that was coming to me, to find patterns and priorities. Surgery had left me with a permanent condition of loud noises continually roaring in my head and, in consequence, a somewhat lowered energy level. Though I longed—and still long—for the complete physical silence I will never know again, I saw in my condition a blessing indeed, an aid to that simplification of life which kept eluding me. All my previous efforts to reduce activities and responsibilities had merely slowed my pace to a fast trot. If there was ever to be a reintegration of my life around my new understandings, it would take nothing less drastic than a year of solitude for this to happen. The sharp break with the past which my physical condition created gave me courage to apply for the necessary leave. It was granted, and this essay is written after my first two months at the hermitage.

My year really began on Christmas day, though I was not able to come up here to stay for another five weeks. The psalm for Tuesday's vespers which I read that day opened the door:

> O Lord, my heart is not proud
> nor haughty my eyes.
> I have not gone after things too great
> nor marvels beyond me.
>
> Truly I have set my soul
> in silence and peace.
> A weaned child on its mother's breast,
> even so is my soul.
>
> O Israel, hope in the Lord
> both now and forever.

Staying clear in my purposes, which involves not setting goals only because they're satisfying and recognizable to others, has required a great deal of effort in the past two months. I do not want to go after things too great, nor marvels beyond me. But the world is excitable, and the

pressures from others to come down from the mountaintop
with a vision, or at least with a set of clay tablets, are
stronger than I would have believed.

Not only do I have to struggle against the expectations
of others, I have had to face my own expectations. There
is no doubt about it, I had fallen into a way of thinking
about the spiritual life which involved hitting upon some
special set of practices that would be a sure recipe for
holiness. By mid-March, I wrote in my journal: "An underlying, slow-growing realization for me in recent days is
that there is no *Way*, no magic Key that will open the Door."

That which we are born remembering, then, is not a
"how to." It is God as Presence. All of prayer, all of meditation, seeks that from which we came, that toward which
we move:

> Thought not to be formed
> Vision not to be seen
> Word not to be heard
> Love not to be known
> God beyond calling
> Be thou my God.

The wisdom of solitude is not easy to translate into the
world. If we arrive in the midst of the old busy scene with
all our being open and vulnerable, we can easily be destroyed. There is a way—and it is my task this year to
learn it—to be present both to God and to the world, and
yet stay shielded.

Learning to live in this new rhythm has involved my
entire family and my working associates. Kenneth has become an increasingly skilled househusband in best twentieth-century liberation style! On Sundays I come to meeting, and go back to town with Kenneth to spend the day
at home there. From time to time members of the family
come up to the family cabin. Periodically I stop at the office
to discuss work with my associate, administrative assistant
and friend, Dorothy Carson, who by managing my contacts
with "the world" has more than any other human being

except my own family contributed to making my new way of life possible.

A spiritual revolutionary has a hard time in our society. The structures of violence and habits of oppression must be destroyed, but by means that we do not yet understand very well. We have only begun to explore the tools of nonviolence and behavioral expressions of love (beyond sex!). It is clear that sociological training can be directed to the exploration of those tools, but in what settings can one do such work today? If much of my work in the future is done from the hermitage, that will not be a denial of society, but an affirmation of what it can become.

Solitude is the most beautiful condition of the human spirit. I understand now what St. Augustine really meant when he said, "Every time I go out among men I return less a man." He was trying to say that in solitude he understood humanness, but easily lost track of it when confronted with his fellow specimens of humanity. I love humans now as I never loved them before when I depended on them daily. It is in solitude that I am learning to truly remember what I have lived forgetting. I hope to learn how to weave the golden threads of solitude into the warp and woof of family and community living. I know of no other way for us to become what we are created to be.

> Solitude I sing for you
> Solitude I pray for you,
> Solitude I do for you.

Postscript: May 5, 1988. Fourteen years later.

"There is a way—and it is my task this year to learn it—," I wrote in 1974, "to be present both to God and to the world, and yet stay shielded." Today I would use the word "centered" rather than "shielded," a word that reflected my intense need for spiritual shelter at that time. Indeed, I found that I was not to stay in solitude or even to remain anchored to the hermitage in between travels and teaching. Rather, I was led from the large state university campus in Boulder to the small college campus of Dartmouth in Hanover, New Hampshire, where I spent my last seven years of teaching before retirement (which I prefer to call "repatterning") in 1985. Those were commuting years, since our house in Boulder remained home. My current repatterning continues to involve some travel and speaking, but also much more time at home in Boulder, picking up the threads of household and local community activity I laid down during the intense years of teaching and international activity. It is very important to me to be "local" as much as possible now.

Not so much time is spent at the hermitage as I anticipated. Not yet. At this stage of our lives, Kenneth seeks the solitude of our family cabin, The Waterfall, more frequently than I. He sometimes stays there, just downhill from the hermitage, for several days at a time. When we are both there we follow the routine we always have followed at The Waterfall: breakfasts separately, lunch and supper together, and a walk in the cool of the evening before retiring to our separate cabins. It is a good rhythm of togetherness and separateness.

My longer stretches of hermitage time are still to come, and they will come. What, in retrospect, did I learn in the year of solitude? That the centering process can be done anywhere when the basic rhythm of living is under control. Outside shielding is not the secret, but an inner ordering. If I allow myself to feel too pressed, I lose the centering. The responsibility to handle pressure is mine, no one else's. People sometimes ask about the roaring inside my head, legacy of the 1973 surgery. It continues, but it is an old friend. It bothers me only when I am very fatigued.

In learning not to rely on shielding, I have gradually been able to develop a discipline of openness to people, to my social environment—a kind of openness I would not have dared to try in my pre-solitude days. I am still very imperfect in the practice of that openness, but I listen more, let more of the outside world in without crowding my inner sense of self, than I used to be able to do. I am older and have less physical and psychic energy than I used to, and therefore need to rest more (I often take after-lunch naps when I am at home). But at the same time I *accept* the world more.

The peak intensity of religious experience has not been maintained, so serious workaday prayer has become more important. What is workaday prayer? It is neither exalted nor anguished, but rather an intentional repeated turning to God. A prayer I devised during my Dartmouth years, walking the mile back and forth between apartment and campus, inwardly sung to the tune of the Tallis Canon, may serve as an example:

> Glory to thee my God the day
> For all the blessings of thy Way;
> Oh keep, oh keep me close to thee
> That I may ever faithful be.

My most constant prayer, the one I say more than any other, is the one I prayed on the way to the operating room in 1973: "Into thy hand, O Lord, I commend my spirit." I don't look for great heights in my prayer life, but I do look for, and experience, connectedness with God.

Kenneth and I are coming to appreciate each other's different spiritualities. While we often seem to travel different tracks, there is a profound sense in which we stand on the same ground, and walk the same path. We are certainly fed from the same source. We need each other. Apart we are incomplete. There is much happiness in the bonds we have woven over the nearly fifty years we have been married, bonds woven out of our likenesses and our differences. What fun, what adventures we have had!— and are still having. While outwardly we are growing deafer, nevertheless the music of the future sounds sweet to the inward ear.

Songs for Our Grandchildren
from Hermitage Hollow

Summer of 1976
The Hermitage
Near Lyons, Colorado

Dear Grandchildren,

When you come to visit us in our house in Boulder we
love to bring you to The Waterfall, our family cabin in the
mountains. A place at The Waterfall you don't see very
often is the hermitage, hidden away out of sight of the
family cabin. It is called the hermitage because it is a cabin
for hermits. Hermits are people who like to live all by
themselves. It is in a little hollow halfway up the steep hill
behind the family cabin. I often go to the hermitage to be
alone for a few days at a time.

I think the hill where the hermitage sits is one of the most
beautiful places in the world. Most of the hill is covered
with forest, but there is also a stretch of meadow across
the hollow. I love to sit on the porch and watch the friends
I write about in these poems, and go for little walks to my
favorite places. On hot summer days I go down to the
waterfall below the hermitage and go for a swim in the
rock pool. At night I sleep on the porch under the stars.
When I live in town I am very busy, but when I am out
here I have lots of time. One of the things I do with the

time I have is to think about my grandchildren, because I love you very much. These poems are written for you because I wanted to share with you the fun of my hermit's life with my forest companions. When you are older I will want to share the other kinds of things I do here, like the putting together of yesterday and tomorrow described in Grandmother's Song. Grandmother's Song is perhaps really more for grownups, but it insisted on being included here.

With very much love,

Grandma

Old Tree

Old tree,
There are secrets
Between you and me.

You sought
Me and here
You've brought me.

In your shade
This house
I've made.

It is good
To live
In solitude.

Yet while here
I'm glad
You're near.

What you know
From years
Of standing so;

Deep-rooted,
In stony soil
Well-suited,

Grown tall
To look
O'er the forest wall—

You'll share
When I'm ready
To hear.

Complaint to a Porcupine

Big fat old porcupine
How is it you can climb
So high in my trees?

You go prowling in the dark,
Strip the forest of its bark
And leave it to freeze.

You are not very pretty.
I think it's a pity
You can go where you please.

I deplore your taste in food,
Still I suppose you do some good
That no one sees.

Ms. Spider

Dear Ms. Spider—
(I sat down beside her)
Why did you spin
Your web so thin
Just over the pool
That shimmers so cool
And invites me in
For a swim?

With my first splash
Your web I'll lash.
I hate to spoil
The fruit of toil.
—I also know
The minute I go
You'll start another
Without any bother!

Sister Deer

Sister Deer, you never come near!
I know that you have much to fear
But I would like to be your friend.
What kind of message can I send?

I know you like the meadow grass
And come here often, but alas
You always lunch by the farthest trees
And at the slightest sound you freeze,

Then plunge and gracefully spring away
Not to return again that day.
Friend deer, my love you cannot know.
Perhaps it's best to leave it so.

God Laughs and Plays

Meister Eckhart says
God laughs and plays.
I know he's right.
All things are bright,
God's presence near
In shy sister deer.
God delights
In the magpie's flights.
Heaven has room
For the cactus in bloom.

God loves butterfly wings
And all mossy things.
She laughs to see
Brer Rabbit and me.
The porcupine
Was her design,
As was Ms. Spider
And the worm beside her,
And the star-specked sky
Where the moon swings by.

Look all around—
It's God's playground!

Grandmother's Song

Oh the memories, the memories.
Who said that life
Could not come twice?
Each new little one
Born to a daughter or to son
Trails the glories
Of older stories.
I remember the morn
When you were born.

Oh the memories, the memories.
And so each sight
Brings twice delight.
Each smile, each word
Echoes unblurred
The Then and Now
Grandmothers know how.

Oh the memories, the memories.
But these are quieter years
With quieter joys and fears.
Old strengths are gone
But we stay on.
New strengths come,
New thoughts in the sun.

Oh the memories, the memories.
Does anyone know what grandmothers dream?
Not as it might seem!
Yesterday melts into tomorrow
Minus human sorrow.
Make the picture clear!
Dream the future while we're here!

Yet always the memories, the memories!
So grandchildren don't be surprised
If we sit with half-closed eyes.
Choose not to work or talk;
Or play, or read, or walk.
We're busy on something new:
A yesterday-tomorrow for you!

Quaker Family Life

Friends Testimonies in the Home

Today, even more than forty years ago when I originally wrote this essay, Quaker families are faced with the problem of maintaining the cherished tradition of the home as a center for social, religious, and some economic activities—in a world that has snatched most of these experiences away from the home. We see many of "the world's" families around us suffering acutely from these losses of function, and we may well ask ourselves, "What kind of family life can we build?" The poet answers, "One small plot of heaven." The Society of Friends also gives some guidance in the matter through its query: "Are you endeavoring to make your home a place of friendliness, refreshment, and peace, where God becomes more real to all who dwell there and to those who visit it?"

Building a home that is a center for the spiritual nourishment of our families and all others who enter it is not easy in our day, living as we do under many kinds of pressure. Yet homes that can provide the bread of heaven as well as earthly bread may be our salvation. Friends historically have had a testimony about this, but it is easier to revere the Quaker family life of the past than to translate these testimonies into modern practices. It is also easy to assume that families of an earlier day didn't have serious conflicts and problems, so harmonious family life was easier to achieve. The devils of two and three hundred years ago wore different costumes than the ones we meet today, but they were just as real. The "domestic bliss" that Thomas Clarkson, a recorder of eighteenth-century Quaker life, considered Friends' chief source of enjoyment was achieved through the same constant effort, devotion, and prayer that we need to put into our own family lives.

We spend so little time in our homes even at best, because of the way modern life is organized, that any additional demands on our time may mean a further weakening of the kind of personal relationships that only common domestic activity can build. In a world crying for a new approach to rapidly multiplying social conflicts, what is the role of the family in untangling our social confusion? A real gap exists between personal spirituality and society-building at the national and international levels. The family stands in this gap.

It is striking that so much of our imagery regarding religious experience is couched in terms of the family: God, loving and forgiving Mother and Father of us all; Jesus, our Teacher and Elder Brother; we, the wayward children united through God in the sisterhood of human-kind. That we first experience the love of God through the love of our parents and that we are able to love God and one another because we have learned to love father and mother and brother and sister is something we tend to ignore. Home is the training ground where people first learn to love, to hate, to get angry, to fear, to forgive. Unless we learn at home how to handle hate, anger, and fear so that it does not destroy ourselves or others, and unless we experience the full depth of forgiveness in the give and take of family life, we are not going to be able to go into the world and help drain off hatreds there.

There are real obstacles to the creation of a home that is a training ground for love and reconciliation. Some of these obstacles lie outside ourselves, in society; others are to be found within. One of the biggest problems that society forces upon us is a confusion about the role of women in today's world. An unfortunate by-product of women's liberation is the view that the real work of the world is done by people who keep office hours, men or women, and that the 24-hour-a-day duty of the homemaker is simply a kind of janitorial work that any simple-minded person could do. Out-achieving men in the marketplace in order to show that women are equal has been the goal of not a few women over the past three decades.

How did women ever get into the position where they felt the need to belittle the amazing experience of bearing and rearing children? Yet already, the women's movement has come full circle, and people are rediscovering the importance of mothering (and fathering). There is now a school of thought, articulated by Sara Ruddick, emphasizing the importance of mothering skills (exercised by both men and women) in the evolution of the social order.

Increasing appreciation of individual differences among women and among men now makes possible a choice of lifeways based on capabilities and preferences. This has made the marriage relationship both richer and more complex. In my youth, a woman expected to adapt her lifeway to that of her spouse. Now the adaptation goes both ways, and parenting is shared in a way we could hardly have imagined in the 1940s.

Yet our educational system has not kept pace with changes in society. While schools are committed in theory to equal education for girls and boys, in practice girls are still "tracked" from preschool on, via the "doll corner" to careers in teaching, nursing, social work, and secretarial work. School gives very mixed messages to female students. They are told to compete at the same time they are taught not to outshine potential future spouses or be too assertive.

Partnering may not initially create a role crisis, since women are now encouraged to pursue careers, but the arrival of children often brings the illusion of equal sharing abruptly to an end. A woman may quite suddenly find herself anchored to the kitchen and nursery. Does she stay there long? Generally not. Preference or economic necessity may send her back into the labor force, although more often than not into dead-end jobs. Then she has the worst of both worlds: an unrewarding job and long extra hours at home with housework and child care which she is too tired to carry out to her own satisfaction. If she is a single parent, the double load is that much heavier. In every country in the world where time-budget studies have been undertaken, women work longer hours than men. They also bear a burden of resentment that things should be so. In the later years of life, women have more time to do other things, but in the young adult years many women feel trapped, enslaved, cheated out of life—instead of enriched by their childbearing.

Men suffer because of the conflict women feel, yet don't often learn the skills that would make them better partners in homemaking. Then there is the husband who is away from home a lot and yet wants to share in the family life when he can be there. He suffers too, because he may find himself shut out from an intimate closed circle of wife and children. The wife has become so efficient at managing without him that there is no role left for him. Where an earlier generation simply accepted such situations, today's young married couples often do not. One or both spouses decide the other is unnecessary, and divorce ensues. This does not happen without great anguish. Generally, each feels betrayed by the other; each had deep needs and high expectations the other did not meet.

Not infrequently, each one of a divorced couple will remarry, and then face the challenge and pain—as well as rewards—of creating a recombined family with parents, children, stepchildren, new relatives, and former spouses. Same-sex marriages are not free of such stress; often there are children from an earlier heterosexual marriage. In addition, there is the pressure of an unfriendly world on a newly created home that does not conform to traditional practices. No matter how much love partners have for one another, such pressures create tensions and conflict.

Another source of conflict stems not from the divided nature of society, but from the divided nature of our own souls. We all harbor unloving feelings inside, leftovers from the process of growing up. Yet our very idealism creates obstacles to working out our personal conflicts. The practice of Christian love and the discipline of the will may not seem compatible with recognition of our own hostile impulses, so we reject their existence without resolving them. Jesus said, "Love thy neighbor as thyself." We can hardly understand and accept our neighbors' obvious shortcomings unless we have first learned to understand and accept our own. Managing our own bad impulses is one of the first steps in the Christian discipline.

This idea is hardly an invention of modern psychology. Jesus' experience in the wilderness with his own temptations is symbolic of an experience we must all go through before we are free to respond to God's promptings. Quaker journals are full of accounts of the struggle with a personal sense of sin; John Woolman's description of his gradual emancipation from his "worldly self" is a touching and classic example. What Quaker mother of today cannot feel for the nameless woman Friend of the eighteenth century who wrote:

> Thy poor friend was never in so low a state as at present, all good has departed from me I fear never to return. What shall I do to be saved? When I go to meeting some silly chatter always prevents the exercise of my known duty. At home I can never be quiet, if I retire from the family it avails me nothing. I cannot collect my thoughts so as to find the cause of this evil, nor can I ever get into a state fit to offer up a petition to Him who alone can help me.

These are some of the conflicts that today's young families face. Some, blessed with rich spiritual resources, congenial temperaments, or similar spousal backgrounds, face the conflicts so quickly and easily that they scarcely realize any problems exist. For others it is a long uphill road to a harmonious relationship and a sense of growing together as a family.

Conflicts *can* be worked out, with the combined help of God and a loving family, if we face them as part of God's direction for us even when we cannot see what the direction is. If our families are to grow in grace, each one of us must take this responsibility for personal resolution of conflict. The miracle of the family is that the resources for strengthening each individual member as well as the whole lie within the family itself. We can be each other's strength.

The working spouse who is away a great deal has a very special task to fulfill despite the limitations of time: offering the homemaking spouse the love and understanding that give strength for carrying on with the work of home and children. The physical and emotional demands of bringing up children, especially during the preschool years, can drive a person to the point of exhaustion. At times like these, love and understanding are more precious than rubies. The spouse who can offer them unfailingly when the point of utter weariness has been reached is taking a real share of the work of childrearing. Sometimes these days, it is the husband who is the homemaking parent; sometimes it is the wife. Often both parents are working, and then the challenge is for each spouse to do their share of homemaking and parenting when both are exhausted.

Whatever the pattern of work inside and outside the home, spouses must help each other find unity and spiritual peace through participation in the wholeness of the family group. Here is the one place where men and women find themselves loved and valued as whole persons. Generally we only meet pieces of people, wherever we go. In social clubs we meet the good-fellow piece of a person; in economic transactions, the business piece; in church, the religious piece; and so on. Other pieces may crowd in on the scene, but the only place any of us is ever a whole person is in the family.

Mutual love and understanding between spouses is the basic strength of any home; the success we have in rearing our children depends largely on the kind of relationship we have with our mate. This makes the first few months of married life pretty important: the time when we develop patterns of living together that either will or won't stand the wear and tear of raising children. People who think that having children will solve their marital problems are tragically misled. Any serious marital conflict is many times intensified by having children. However, if a couple has a basically good relationship, the inevitable difficulties that childrearing bring will result in real spiritual growth for them both. An expanding family brings an expanding capacity for happiness.

We are always so concerned with how we can help our children that we sometimes fail to realize how much our children are helping us, or how much they could help us if we let them. My husband and I have frequently been reminded that we can never give our children (and now our grandchildren) half of what they have given us. Because they are so sensitive, and respond so quickly to our unspoken as well as spoken thoughts, they show us much about ourselves that we would otherwise not have known.

If we use our children's reactions as a guide, instead of as a springboard for our own tempers, we can ourselves develop increased sensitivity to *their* needs (along with better self-control). This sensitivity to the needs of others is the greatest gift our children can give us, along with a capacity to see the world anew and relish things too long taken for granted. One of the greatest contributions that men and women with their childrearing years behind them can make to the community is to put that increased sensitivity to work in community service. But parents can gain this increased awareness of others only if they allow their children, and then their grandchildren, to be their teachers.

Another source of strength available to the family has unfortunately often become a source of tension: I refer to grandparents. Today's seniors raised their children to value independence and individualism more than anything else. Now they are finding that these children, now parents themselves, have difficulty making a real place in their family group for grandparents. This is happening at a time when life expectancy has dramatically increased, and there are many more seniors among us than there used to be. Even where grandparents never consciously taught their children such individualism, society was at work molding the new family pattern and whittling down the size of the dwelling unit to the point where the spare room is non-existent. The possible reasons for conflict between generations in any particular family may be numerous indeed. Some lucky families have little such conflict. But where it exists, the main hope for overcoming conflict lies in the growing spiritual maturity of both parents and grandparents. Knowing our own inadequacies more accurately, we will not be so quick to point up the inadequacies of the other generation. This liberates us all to accept the warmth and love and wisdom that can flow between generations.

Love alone does not solve all family problems. Intellectual understanding can be very helpful in facing family difficulties. Simplistic formulas for childrearing have fallen somewhat into disrepute as a result of the radical shifts in recent decades from strict schedules and strict discipline to demand schedules and the child-centered home, and now back again to "tough love." Specialists change their minds from time to time. This affects parents in different ways. Some feel safer using their own common sense; others become very dependent on the latest specialist's advice. In general, however, the parents who have been led astray by the specialists are the ones who are looking for a formula by which to raise their children. If we look at current work in child psychology with an intelligently critical attitude, realizing there are no simple patterns into which one can fit a child's behavior, we can find certain approaches to conflict situations that are of great value.

One important contribution of the peace movements of the sixties and seventies was to turn our attention to conflict resolution and peacemaking in the family setting. Among Friends, publications such as *Sharing Space,* a newsletter from the Children's Creative Response to Conflict Program in Nyack, New York, and the manuals published by the Nonviolence and Children Program of Philadelphia Yearly Meeting have empowered families and communities to deal with conflict creatively. Many Friends also use James and Katherine McGinnis's *Parenting for Peace and Justice,* and the family conflict resolution programs of the St. Louis Institute for Peace and Justice.

Every home built on love and understanding works out its own ways of coming to decisions and dealing with the apparently conflicting desires of different family members. Some families hold formal family councils; others use a more informal approach. The chief value of a more formal type of family council is that each person is assured of a chance to speak while others listen.

The mutual give and take of family life does not require that each of us give exactly fifty percent and take exactly fifty percent. Most families face problems for which there is no "mathematically" correct answer. They may even face a situation in which an individual feels a call that makes it impossible to serve the best interests of the family in the usual sense of that term. Every Christian home needs to be sensitive to the implications of this hard passage in the gospel of Luke: "If any one comes to me without turning his back on his father and mother and wife and children and brothers and sisters, indeed his very self, he cannot be my follower" *(Luke 14:26)*. This command I take as symbolic of the intensity of God's call to us.

Each one of us has a special calling. Many psychosociological and physiological explanations can be invoked, but the fact remains that each one of us, because of who and what we are at this moment, has a special way to serve God. The very qualities that make us able to answer an important call may make us insensitive to basic needs in our immediate family. Some of the qualities that made Gandhi able to give dedicated and disciplined leadership to great masses of people in India prevented him from recognizing his responsibility for the spiritual welfare of his own family. Not until his later years did he realize he had forced on his wife and children a way of life that can only properly come through an act of personal acceptance and choice. Not many couples face the very dramatic conflicts that Gandhi so honestly describes in his autobiography, but we all face them to some degree, however slight. Today, with our heightened sense of the worth of every man and woman, we no longer easily accept that women must discipline themselves to be more sensitive to the

needs of their families than men. We no longer take it for
granted that women must bear the full burden, as did
Gandhi's wife, of making the necessary adjustments to
achieve a sense of spiritual harmony in the family. Yet
situations arise in which one spouse—it may be either
one—is indeed called upon to bear that burden.

Each of us has certain blind spots. They may be the
by-product of a great sense of mission, or simply the result
of some crippling emotional experience in the past. The
blind spots may not affect our general adjustment to the
outside world at all, and yet make for problems in the
family. Every spouse must accept, compensate for, and
cover with love some part of their partner's family behavior
that may be inadequate. The real test of a healthy family
life is whether each spouse is able to love and protect the
weak spots of the other. If the partners can only blame
each other for their weaknesses, the time may have come
to turn to outside help. The family that tries to build on
anything less than the rock of acceptance of each family
member *as is* cannot provide for the spiritual growth and
well-being of its members.

Each of us who feels called to take a position on a public
issue that is not in conformity with the world's view feels
the weight of conflicting pressures, no matter how firmly
the conviction is held. When such a position is taken by
a family, the weight is in some ways lightened but in other
ways made heavier. It is lightened because sharing unusual
views with our nearest and dearest gives us tremendous
emotional support and strength. Most of us are not aware
of the extent to which we value the approval of our own
family until we get into a tight spot and find unexpected
support at home. But young children cannot understand
and carry out an unpopular witness with the same clarity
that adults can. Their time perspective and life experiences
are limited, so they are much more vulnerable to opposing
pressures. The family thus confronts a double problem:

the impact of the outside world on the child, and the way the child relates to the family in the face of this impact. Such challenges are faced primarily by nonconformist families bearing their testimony in a community that does not share their views. Many of the problems raised here do not exist for those families who already live in communities committed to a different way of life. One of the greatest values of intentional communities is that they support children as well as adults in nonconformity.

Since nonconformity brings with it real burdens, particularly to the young who are least able to bear them, it is important that Friends consider their testimonies prayerfully, making sure they are always testifying to essentials, to things that really matter. Children who are compelled to conform to observances that have little meaning to them frequently revolt against all the values associated with those observances. We have in fact come to regard the revolt of young people as a value in itself, and the Society of Friends has always received much of its strength from the influx of such young people who have rejected the ways of their own family and church. Revolt looks different, however, when we consider the other side of the coin: the possibility of our own children rejecting Quaker ways!

One reason the Society of Friends dwindled so rapidly after an initial period of expansion was because it overemphasized many outward practices not related to the essential spirit of Quaker testimonies. In earlier days, many family crises revolved around use of "the world's" dress and language, attendance at musical concerts, and other dangerous diversions. Disownment or voluntary abandonment of Friends' ways often hinged on these issues. Today, family crises tend to revolve around television, rock concerts, and punk haircuts. Friends faced with these problems might well ponder Margaret Fell's words to early Friends regarding undue concern with outward things:

> This narrowness and strictness is entering in, that many cannot tell what to do, and not to do. Poor Friends is mangled in their minds, that they know not what to do; for one Friend says one way, and another, another . . . they say we must look at no col-

ours, nor make anything that is changeable colours as the hills are, nor sell them nor wear them. But we must be all in one dress, and one colour. This is a silly poor gospel. It is more fit for us to be covered with God's eternal Spirit, and clothed with his eternal Light, which leads us and guides us into righteousness and to live righteously and justly and holily in this present evil world.

This does not *answer* the question of what to do in these various perplexing situations. There is no formula, and families who try to live by a formula are often the ones who run into trouble. Our aim is to help our children grow "righteously and justly and holily" into adulthood, not to enforce immediate compliance with specific attitudes while they are children. Each home must find its own solution. What can the family honestly ask of its members? What are the members honestly willing to accept? Far more important than a particular solution is the spirit in which it is reached. We cannot always make decisions for our children. We can only hope to accustom them to turning to their Inward Teacher when decisions have to be reached.

Elizabeth Fry's experience in this regard is very revealing. She tried to force her own children into the strict mold of the Quakerism of her day, forgetting that she herself had had a gay and free youth in which to work off all her high spirits. She came to Quakerism of her own free will and accepted gladly the disciplines the Society imposed, regarding them as aids to spiritual growth. But her children had no such choice. They saw the delights of the world constantly from the sidelines, particularly as their mother's work drew her into the highest worldly circles, but they were forbidden to taste them. As a result, only one of the ten children who lived to maturity remained a Friend.

In the wisdom of her old age, Elizabeth wrote:

> The longer I live, the more difficult do I see education to be; more particularly as it respects the religious restraints that we put upon our children. To do enough and not too much is a most delicate and important point. I begin seriously to doubt whether as it respects the peculiar scruples of Friends, it is not better quite to have sober-minded young persons to judge for themselves. I have such a fear that in so much mixing religion with those things that

are not delectable, we may turn them from the thing itself. I see, feel and know that where these scruples are adopted from principle, they bring a blessing with them, but where they are only adopted out of conformity to the views of others, I have very serious doubts whether they are not a stumbling block.

She recorded later in her journal that when she was able to accept her grown children as people in their own right and not as stubborn clay to be molded, she began for the first time enjoying the feeling that she and her children were *friends*.

The *spirit* of our faith is the best thing we can give our children. Our daily conduct and attitudes toward all the events that impinge on the family will convey much more to the children than all the preaching in the world. They may learn more from the way we treat troublesome neighbors than from wrapping and sending a dozen parcels abroad.

The home does not, and cannot, bear entirely alone the responsibility for the nurture of its children in a special way of life. Relating to and identifying with a community that gives moral support to the family's way of life is important for each family member. For most people, the geographical community is the community of identification. For nonconformists, it often is not. The community to which the nonconformist looks for support is a community of like-minded people which may be scattered all over the earth. Thus the Quaker community is the Society of Friends, the pacifist community is for some the Fellowship of Reconciliation, for others the War Resisters' League, and so on. Many Quakers and pacifists do belong to a small local community such as a Friends meeting which meets their need for support, but many others live in isolation from like-minded people. Those who live in isolation must establish their sense of community through correspondence, reading, and occasional conferences. Everyone needs a community of like-minded people to belong to.

If this is true of adults, how much more true it is of children! Mature persons have had a lifetime of opportunity to develop an inner direction which may be independent of the actions of those immediately around them, but children have yet to develop this sense and are much more influenced by what goes on around them. Quaker families with small children especially need the security of a Friends meeting, preferably with other young children in it, which supports their "differentness." A pacifist family that stands alone in a patriotic community, particularly in a time of war fever, places a heavy burden on young children. I remember suffering with my elementary-school-age children during the Korean war over the issue of buying war stamps in the schools.

Children of families that stand alone benefit greatly by attending conferences, summer camps, yearly meetings, and any other special Quaker or pacifist gatherings that include children. These activities give children reassurance that their own family is not completely off base. I have often observed the delight of parents and the relief of children attending a Quaker family camp in a predominantly non-Quaker area, as they discover that other families are bringing up their children in similar ways.

We should not feel too sorry for ourselves as members of a minority group, however. Sociologists have observed that members of minority groups can, under certain conditions, have a tremendous advantage over the conforming majority of our society. Since the majority have no highly specific standards by which to judge their own behavior, they are dependent on shifting public opinion to determine their actions. In trying to go with an uncertain flow, they often end by pleasing nobody, least of all themselves. The minority group tends to have more clearly defined standards; while there may be occasions of uncertainty about the proper course of action, they at least have one primary standard to refer to and are not trying to satisfy values that are in constant flux. Their lives have an integration and a purposefulness that are much more important than superficial adjustment to the mainstream of society. Achieving this integration at maturity is well worth the conflict that children may experience before they can identify themselves with the special standards of their group.

Perhaps the most trying period for the child in the non-conformist home is adolescence, although each age brings its own difficulties. Since adolescence in our society is typically a period of revolt and a time of strong identification with one's own age group to the exclusion of parents, young people whose parents want them to be "different" clearly face an acute conflict at this time. In a community where they can't belong to a crowd that shares these differences, they will be equally miserable whether they choose to stand with their parents or stick with their peers. There can be no comfortable resolution of this problem. At the same time, where there has always been a sound and happy relationship between parents and children, the children have much less need to revolt.

A Quaker boarding school can sometimes help ease the child through this period without the necessity for revolt. Here the adolescent has an opportunity to be one of the gang in a setting where the "different" way is the normal way. There is an opportunity to think through the implications of pacifism and nonmaterialistic goals without feeling strong pressures either to rebel or to conform. Young people can have the experience of discovering these truths for themselves. This experience of discovery is essential and can take the place of rebellion. However, there are many arguments against sending a child out of the family at the early age of thirteen. Closely knit families with a strong sense of shared values may not want to consider this as even a remote possibility. Whether our children remain at home or go away to school, we will have served them truly and well if we can have enough faith in them and in the power of the Spirit to leave them free to make their own discovery of truth.

One of the most important things we can do for our children from the time of their earliest childhood is to understand and accept the struggles they will almost inevitably go through. We shouldn't minimize the suffering a child feels, no matter how insignificant the cause appears to us. If a child has been bullied or teased or ganged up on by other children, we don't help them if we say, "Oh, never mind those bullies," or, "No matter what happens, don't you ever hit back." Without being oversolicitous, we must recognize the *reality for them* of the suffering they go through. If we scold them for their emotional reactions or deny their pain—"That didn't really hurt!"—they may begin to feel ashamed of and repress their feelings. Such repressed feelings pile up through the years and make each conflict situation they face harder to deal with, burdened as they are with hostile feelings of which they are no longer conscious. This principle of letting children know their troubles are understood is important for any parent, but how much more so for those who seek to bring up their children to love their enemies!

Another thing we can do for our children is help them anticipate and prepare for the tight spots in which they may find themselves. We know that a small child can be helped to face a painful hospital experience by playing out the situation in advance at home, with the doctor, nurses, operating table, strange bedroom, bandages, and likelihood of pain all brought into the play. Similarly, during the years of conscription, many conscientious objectors found it extremely helpful to hold mock tribunals and practice stating their case before a mock board of unsympathetic examiners. We should be imaginative about seizing opportunities for acting out at home difficult situations that our adolescents may find themselves in if they are trying to uphold the peace testimony.

So far, I have emphasized the differences between the nonconformist home and the larger community, and ways we can maintain these differences. However, we also have a responsibility to maintain positive relationships beyond the home. Family life is after all a preparation for our participation in the greater human community. A family that simply succeeds in maintaining itself intact in splendid isolation from the local community would be like a host who prepared a great banquet and then sat down and ate it alone instead of inviting in the guests.

Hospitality is the great avenue of relationship to the community. Monotonous cocktail parties and silent television evenings have replaced the relaxed congenial conversation of earlier times when people depended more on their own resources for entertainment. A home that has the courage to provide the simple old-fashioned entertainment of good conversation will find its hospitality eagerly sought. Young people particularly enjoy having a home they can come to and use freely as a social center, knowing that the adults there are their friends and care about what is happening to them. It is not unusual for the nonconformist home to become a real community center, because people appreciate so much the opportunity to visit with one another in the atmosphere of genuine warmth that such homes often provide. The frequent exercise of such hospitality opens up possibilities for the mixing of people of different races, religions, and political ideas in an environment where they can be open to one another.

Participating in the kind of community activities that one can conscientiously support is very important. However, Friends and others who have chosen a nonconformist way of life must constantly remind ourselves that our ways appear different not because we wish to set ourselves apart as a peculiar people, but because we wish to be part of a universal kinship in a deeper, more meaningful sense than is possible through ordinary types of community relationships. There may be times when we should do as George Fox did on one memorable occasion—"smoke a pipe of tobacco," that others may know we have unity with all Creation. If we live in the right spirit, our nonconformity will draw us closer to our fellow human beings, not farther away from them.

The testimonies of the Society of Friends have from the beginning been considered as concerns of the individual and of the meeting, but rarely have they been considered at the family level. Howard Brinton's summary of the testimonies under the headings of community, harmony, equality, and simplicity in the Pendle Hill Pamphlet entitled *The Nature of Quakerism* gives us four useful categories for checking out the state of our "family witness."

The Testimony of Community

The family is the primary community in which we live. With so many outside activities to pull each member away, however, it is easy to forget that the home is more than bedroom and dining room. Not everything that is done within the family circle is particularly sacred and valuable, but family well-being depends upon doing a certain number of things together.

While family chores give each person a sense of responsibility for the maintenance of the home, these chores are quite frequently matters of individual activity. One family I know, feeling the need of more group activity, has made weekly cleaning a group project. On Saturday mornings, all gather and work through the house as a crew until the cleaning is done. Family members actually look forward each week to the singing and laughing that accompany the scrubbing. Recreative activity within the family group is also increasingly rare. Some families have developed absorbing hobbies, along musical, scientific, or craft lines. Anna Brinton recalled that her grandmother used to do difficult mathematical problems for recreation in the minutes she could snatch each day from her household cares.

However, not all families have such specialized interests or skills. Most of us need to think in terms of what things we might profitably do together that have previously been done alone—as in the case of the joint cleaning project. Reading aloud together can become a valued family tradition. One friend recalls that her mother read aloud to the children on summer evenings while they prepared vegetables for canning. In the days when ironing was more a part of women's chores than it is now, husbands read aloud to their wives during an evening of ironing. There are many possibilities for combining recreation and work. Traveling in the car can be an adventure or a source of intense irritation, depending on family resourcefulness in inventing car games. What families do together should be fun.

How can we develop ways in which the family as a group can express its concerns for the world community? Most of our social action work is done as individuals on committees. It is rare for children to participate, and partners may feel left out of activities in which they would like to share. Family-to-family relationships established across racial lines can do more to change basic attitudes in a community than all the committee meetings in the world. Similarly, correspondence with families in sister cities on other continents can involve the whole family in building bridges of peace.

The Testimony of Harmony

The testimony of harmony, more frequently called the peace testimony, was implicit in our discussion of family tensions. Howard Brinton wrote:

> Peaceableness exists as a positive power by which an inner appeal is made to the best that is in man, rather than as an external pressure by forces from outside him. This must include that kind of love and understanding which integrates separate and conflicting elements into a higher unity.

Our first experiences of the power of this inner appeal occur within the family circle.

Well-meaning parents sometimes hesitate to introduce the concept of pacifism to their children at an early age because they doubt it can be understood. While it is true that children can't be expected to use adult techniques of reconciliation in their brief but stormy squabbles, parents shouldn't underestimate what children can absorb from example and even discussion at a very early age. Many years ago our preschool-age son taught us a good lesson in this respect. His two-year-old brother had just torn in two a picture he particularly valued. I plunged into the situation immediately, both to retrieve the picture in hopes that it could be pasted together, and to protect the youngest from the violent revenge I expected to follow. But four-year-old Russell looked up at me calmly and said, "Mother, we're Quakers." And then, thoughtfully, "But Mark's a Quaker too!" As if to say, why doesn't he behave like one! What train of thought led to that peaceful reaction at that particular moment I do not know. But it was clear that he had for a moment a new perception of a situation that would ordinarily have called for violence. I hoped that the frequency of such perceptions would increase as he grew older, and they did!

The Testimony of Equality

The testimony of equality is not easy to apply in a constructive manner. To say that equality means equality of opportunity only states the problem; it does not solve it. Each family must work through to an understanding of what kinds of opportunities are compatible with the welfare of the group as a whole.

The testimony of equality is especially difficult to apply now that the two-career family is becoming the norm. Responsibility for care of the home has to be shared not only between spouses, but with children. Beyond this, there is the challenge of supporting each family member in following her own bent. Again, equality of opportunity has to be interpreted in some meaningful way. The family council can be a constructive way of including children in the process of deciding what's fair. This does not give children's wishes free rein at the expense of parents' needs, but helps them see their own desires in relation to the total family picture. In such a setting, the younger members are often able to moderate exorbitant demands to an extent that surprises parents unused to sharing their problems with their children.

The Testimony of Simplicity

The testimony for simplicity is perhaps most widely discussed in relation to family life, yet it is difficult to translate into a satisfactory pattern of living. What *is* simplicity? If it is the absence of superfluity, by what standard do we judge what is superfluous? It is impossible to get any real agreement on what outward forms simplicity should take. Early Friends were much concerned with the outward forms of simplicity, such as dress, modes of speech, and the absence of aesthetic distractions such as music and art. But even in that early period, Margaret Fell recognized that undue observance of outward things led into separateness instead of toward unity with all creation:

> Away with these whimsical, narrow imaginations, and let the Spirit of God which he hath given us, lead us and guide us; and let us stand fast in that liberty wherewith Christ hath made us free, and not be entangled again into bondage, in observing proscriptions in outward things, which will not profit or cleanse the inward man.

The implication here is clear: simplicity is essentially a spiritual quality, and not a special attribute of any outward way of life. Some people who have a comfortable share of this world's goods create an atmosphere of unhurried serenity and simplicity in their homes. Others who live in rigorous physical simplicity may have homes that are in a of perpetual confusion. In considering how to achieve simplicity in our homes, we must ask ourselves what things are standing between us and the inward life of the spirit we are trying to achieve. For some people, almost all material possessions are a real burden, and they can only follow their light if their physical surroundings are of the simplest compatible with health and cleanliness. Others find that the presence of beautiful objects, paintings, and generally colorful surroundings are a help and inspiration to their inward life. Each one of us must seek to create the environment in our homes that will most "profit or cleanse the inward person."

We should not simply dismiss the attitude of early Friends toward music and art as narrow or old-fashioned. Their basic concern was that Friends should not be turned away from their true calling by distracting diversions. Anything in our lives that diverts us from what we feel our true calling to be should be examined most carefully. However, a *right* use of music and art can be as true an expression of the love of God as an act of prayer or outward service. The same is true of the *right* use of recreation, which is, literally, a *re-creation* of the human spirit. The use of labor-saving devices should be considered in the same light.

No discussion of simplicity is complete without a consideration of its application to the complexity of our social life, using "social" in its broadest sense. Friends are apt to feel the burden of the world's suffering so keenly that they are tempted to participate in almost every activity that comes to their attention which aims to alleviate some of that suffering. The resulting busyness of their lives often reduces them to a state of exhausted frustration. Duties performed out of a sense of compulsion rather than a sense of love are what early Friends called "creaturely activity." If times of inward retirement were so essential to Jesus, who perpetually lived and moved in God's presence, how much more important they should be to us, lacking such constant sensitivity to the motions of the Spirit.

Worship in the Home

This leads us directly into a consideration of the place of worship in the home. If we accept the act of worship as having central significance in our lives, a weekly experience of corporate worship is not enough. Each individual has to face the problem of how to find time for private devotions in a busy day. Those who consider worship important enough to make a specific plan for it are most apt to succeed in having a daily period of inward retirement. The practice of private devotion, or a time of shared

devotion in which partners both participate, is basic to any
sense of dedicated family life. Families can fulfill the high
calling outlined in the early part of our discussion only if
parents make themselves receptive to a daily inflowing of
divine love.

The devotional practices of parents, however, are only
a part of the religious life of the family. Worship experiences with our children must complete the wholeness of
our family life. The love that family members feel for one
another on occasions of special rejoicing can be a key that
will unlock the very doors of heaven; every family should
seize moments of great family joy to turn for a moment in
prayer to the Source of all joy. Birthdays, holidays, times
when good news has come to the family—these can be
opportunities for a spontaneous verbal or silent expression
of gratitude for the ever-present love of God. (Times of
sorrow should also be times of prayer, but unfortunately
we need to be reminded more about the prayer of joy than
the prayer of sorrow.) When such moments are seized,
small children will have an *experience* of prayer that may
be harder for them to gain in more formalized periods.

A regular daily period of family worship was taken for
granted in every Christian home in the generations previous to my own. By the time of World War II, such periods
were the exception rather than the rule. Even when it was
earnestly desired by the parents, it was reluctantly given
up. For the most part, children so obviously regarded it
as an unpleasant chore that parents realized they were
somehow mixing religion with "those things that are not
delectable." Most families felt—rightly—that forcing a worship period on unwilling children was hardly conducive
to the development of their spiritual life. It is possible,
however, that we have given up too easily on this matter
of family worship; we have not been imaginative enough
about the ways in which such worship can be conducted.
What family, habitually beginning the meal with a moment
of worship, has not at some time been caught up in a
wonderful spirit of love during that moment, and perhaps
recognized the children as the source of the uplift? One of

the most memorable worship experiences in our own family came one day when we sat down to a picnic lunch in the back yard. As we bowed our heads, our three-year-old said, "Let's have the birds sing grace for us today." They did, most beautifully! We know also, from the Quaker journals, that children under seven sometimes had profound religious openings which they remembered all their lives.

But it is not enough simply to be sensitive to opportunities for spontaneous worship when they arise. The groundwork for the dedicated lives we wish to lead comes from conscious daily spiritual discipline. If we depended on moments of exaltation to carry us through the daily task of living, we wouldn't be carried very far! How, then, can we help our children turn toward God on their own initiative?

In our own experience, we came gradually to realize that what we called family worship was increasingly becoming parent's worship, since we had followed the usual practice of Bible reading and silence. The three-year-old who was willing to sit quietly in his mother's lap became an adventurous four-year-old who found the morning quiet a period of confinement and irritation. At first I was glad that I was able to close my eyes and center down in spite of his irritability and desire to distract me, but suddenly one day it came to me that we were excluding him from the very experience we most wanted him to have. There was certainly no family unity growing out of this daily period of exclusion. Shortly afterward, we tried not taking the Bible down from the shelf at all for a week, and even the youngest entered into this with real joy. Mornings were begun in a spirit of love and unity, and every one of us felt spiritually refreshed in a way we had not been before. In trying to meet the children's needs more adequately we found that we were meeting our own more adequately too. When at the end of the week we brought out the Bible with the intention of reading a psalm we thought the four-year-old would really enjoy, his immediate response was, "Oh, let's not have worship out of the book!" Little Russell knew what Jesus meant when he said, "God is a spirit, and they that worship Him, must worship in spirit and in truth" *(John 4:24).*

Those with preschool-age children may temporarily find that in spite of their most earnest efforts, family worship does not fit into the daily schedule. The arrival of a new baby, serious illness, or a period of hyperactivity on the part of the children—any of these and more may keep us from our daily appointment. During such a period in our family the winter our third baby arrived, I suddenly realized that the silent periods before meals were becoming a little longer and more meaningful to the children. Was it too much to hope that they also felt a need? If we never lose the sense of need, we will return to the family worship as we can, and in the meantime, God understands and forgives. When we were ready to resume our regular family gathering after Christie's birth, the Hindu student who had been sharing our home for the year suggested we use lighted candles during the silence to help quiet the children and focus their attention on thoughts of God. We tried it, at first successfully, but after several evenings the restlessness was increasing rather than decreasing. In discussing the matter with our eldest, who was by then five, we asked what we could do to help him and the younger ones use the silence for real prayer. Would he like pictures, flowers, music—since candles were no longer enjoyed? He looked at me pityingly and said, "Mother, why don't we just have silence?" And I learned again what I needed to be taught so many times: that we must not strive unduly for the things of the spirit.

The adolescent period may be very difficult in terms of the shared religious life of the family. Parents may feel rebuffed as young people assert their independence in areas that have formerly been fully shared, and believe they are now facing the irreparable consequences of mistakes they have made in their earlier relationships with the children. A wise friend who came to that stage before we did pointed out the necessity for parents to recognize opportunities in the new kind of relationship that develops during adolescence. For the first time, young people are standing off and looking their parents over with a really critical eye. Instead of shrinking under this critical gaze, this is the time for parents to deepen their own spiritual lives. If we parents can grow sufficiently through that most critical testing period, and can continue to grow all our lives, we may come into spiritual fellowship with our children when they are adults. And what a joy it is when we hold their babies in our arms, and begin the spiritual journey anew with the next generation.

The practice of praying individually with the children at their bedtime has fortunately stood the test of time in most families better than family worship has. I began this practice with each of my children at birth, and other parents have felt as I do that prayer is as important to the tiny infant's growth as milk. Toddlers contribute to the prayer as their vocabulary develops. The act of holding up the events of the day in prayer before the Heavenly Parent as well as the earthly parents enables children to go to sleep with a sense of release and security.

Home is where our witness as Friends begins. Each family must work out its own patterns of behavior according to the needs and capacities of its members. This is true most of all in religious practice. If we fail to be sensitive to individual temperaments and needs in this vital area of our lives, we may turn those we love from that which we most long for them to have. We must remember in everything we do as families, from the humdrum to the exciting to the peak inspirational moments, that the ultimate goal is to enable each of us to live close to the Source of all goodness and love, "in the virtue of that life and power that takes away the occasion of all wars."

Families as Centers of Peace and Love: Paradoxes and Contradictions

Nearly forty years after I wrote *Friends Testimonies in the Home*, I sat down to consider the same theme: families as centers of peace and love. The paradoxes and contradictions of the late 1980s present an altered social context for the same question I asked in 1951: "Is your home a center of peace and love for all who enter therein?" What follows are some views on Quaker concerns about the family that I have collected through correspondence and meeting discussions. I found a very new question in many minds. In fact, I was taken aback by the vehemence, the intensity, of a concern about violence—not just in the world, but in Quaker families.

As someone who joined marriage and Quakerism simultaneously a few short months before the U.S. entered World War II, I have worked at the challenge of applying the Quaker peace testimony in the family for my entire life. *Friends Testimonies in the Home* had been written when only three of our five children had been born. The circle of young Ann Arbor Meeting parents which was our support group through the birthing and rearing of those five children must have spent hundreds of hours over the years talking about how to practice both spiritual and physical nonviolence in the home, and how to rear our children to be peacemakers in the larger world. Our conversations always assumed that home was the starting point for the practice of nonviolence, that it was the first training ground. If anything, my feeling about the importance of the family as training ground has intensified over the years as my understanding of what constitutes a family has been steadily strengthened.

There was never a running away from the fact of conflict. Conflict between spouses and between parents and children, difficulties finding the right approach for handling anger nonviolently, were fully acknowledged. But conflict was always discussed in terms of *nonviolence*. The unasked question then was, what about violence when it occurs? Today the big question, for those who are willing to discuss it, is not whether there *is* violence in Quaker families, but whether there is more or less violence than in other families.

How could I, and my generation generally in the Society of Friends, have missed this question? Certainly the violence did not begin yesterday. Willful blindness to unpleasant facts is not an adequate explanation, although there is some truth to the willful blindness theory. In the early 1940s I interviewed Iowa women whose husbands had been sent overseas, to find out how they were managing home and children alone. I often saw whips and sticks in kitchen corners, and the women freely admitted using them as the most effective discipline available to them. But in my heart I didn't really believe that these generally cheerful and friendly women actually used those whips. To this day I have never seen a child whipped, or a woman beaten.

Statistics on child abuse and wife abuse in the general society have been widely published, and such figures on abuse in Quaker families are now available. It has taken a strong effort of the will to assimilate this information in the same way that I have assimilated information about violence in Vietnam, or Northern Ireland, or Lebanon, or India, or Central America. And yet this is also violence I have never seen. Why do I resist the one and not the other? Perhaps because domestic violence does not match my map of the world. Many of us are operating with outdated maps, and it is time we took some lessons in social geography.

At another and deeper level, I wonder if we in the Society of Friends do not have a particular kind of spiritual problem. Every major religion uses the family as a metaphor for our relationship with one another and the Creator in the created order. However, the metaphor has been used in two very different senses. In one, God is the stern patriarch who punishes his children with suffering and sometimes death when they disobey. Many stories from the Old Testament testify to this. If this Divine Patriarch is taken as a spiritual model, violence is justified at home and abroad as a necessary part of calling people to goodness. In the other sense, God is our loving Mother/Father, tender and nurturing. That nurture has been made flesh in the Holy Family for Christians, and stands as the template for nonviolence in the western world. The Bible gives us both families, and both are imprinted in our hearts in ways that defy rational analysis.

There is no question about Friends' strong conscious intellectual and spiritual commitment to the nurturing model. But I suggest that the continued coexistence of both models at a deep level of our awareness creates opportunities for self-deception for Quakers. We slip back and forth between models without realizing it; in this way both violent and nonviolent behaviors can be unconsciously rationalized This self-deception is further aided for some, perhaps many, by the very real experience of having dealt with bitter conflict through prayer, and finding spiritual resources that give strength to *cope* with conflict without resort to violence. What often remains is a residue of hidden emotional turbulence along with a fierce commitment to behavioral nonviolence. The self-deception lies in the unacknowledged residue of anger. It can show in violently nonviolent silence—a perversion of Quaker silence if ever there was one! The more anger is repressed, the more emotional investment there is in maintaining the appearance of nonviolence. Thus the patriarchal God lives on.

For those who cannot maintain their own standard but

succumb to violence or are its victims, the need to maintain the appearance of the nurturing model must be even stronger. The fact that most Quakers belong to a protected middle-class sector of society further aids the self-deception. We have created a fictive social reality about family life to match our Quaker teachings, and it is taking a new generation to challenge that fictive reality.

Self-deception may be too harsh a term, but I use it out of a deep respect for those who are struggling to awaken Quakers to the fact that violence exists not only in the outside world, but in our own Society as well. Friends are very resistant to this message. The first-ever workshop on violence in Quaker families held at Pendle Hill in 1986 may signal the beginning of a new openness to this problem.

I am convinced that our continued spiritual growth as a Society, and the effectiveness of our work in the world, depend in our nuclear era on a deeper understanding of the workings of violence in the heart. New mechanisms, new strategies, new social arrangements can do little by themselves to ensure a continuing human society on the planet if we do not learn how to rechannel the energies that repeatedly drive us to hurt one another. The lion will never lie down with the lamb on a "let's pretend" basis, and perhaps too much of what we do as Quakers is "let's pretend."

In what follows I will examine further the concerns that have been expressed to me about the contradictory experiences of family life, and then introduce some sociological perspectives. Next I will raise again the old question each Quaker generation has asked: How *do* we make our homes centers of peace and love? The answers I have found among concerned Friends may help lay the basis for a realistic peace praxis in today's Quaker families.

Friends' strong and continuing affirmation of the family as a source of strength and joy to each member, and as the vital source of meeting energy, should never be underestimated. Friends speak of how much the multigenerational aspect of Quaker life means to them. Many Quaker events are for all ages, and do not involve leaving children at home with sitters. This means that Quaker families can do more things together than many other families: shared silence in meeting for worship, shared recreation, shared social action. Quarterly meeting, yearly meeting, and other special gatherings are *family* gatherings. Yet some Friends are concerned that we do too much special programming for children at these intergenerational events, thus losing the best of the sharing. How much of such programming is out of concern for the children, and how much is a desire to keep children out of the way?

Parents speak of the abundance of resources Quaker teachings provide for family living—in particular the Quaker teaching about discovering that of God in everyone. It creates a gentle, divine pressure to seek the best in one another in family interaction, and is an important preparation for relating to others in the outside world. The sense of the family as a place where one is accepted and loved for oneself, a place from which to go out into the world and a place to come back to, is not unique to Friends. The family is, however, more important to groups trying to live a different way of life. It literally becomes a sanctuary, and Friends value the family as just that. It is also seen as the source of strength that enables one to engage actively in community life.

Side by side with these affirmations of family life as a source of acceptance and strength come complaints that the family can be a source of stress in the attempt to practice Quaker testimonies outside the home. Every age since the founding of Quakerism has seen its own forms of social turbulence and unrest as the Pandora's Box of industrialization has released one evil after another into the modern world. In the twentieth century, strains under the threat of nuclear war, environmental degradation, and growing social and economic inequalities have been particularly heavy. The demands for social action in the light of Quaker testimonies are very great, and many find that family needs hinder and distract them from attending to pressing social needs. Others experience a pressure for social witness which devalues the family, and feel guilty when spending time on family togetherness.

Lack of time to meet both family and community needs is a great problem. Parents feel that this lack of time means they do not deal adequately with the pressures of materialism, that they do not attend enough to the individuality of each child, that they do not engage in enough listening dialogue in the home, and, specifically, that they do not spend enough time teaching and practicing nonviolence. Single-parent families feel these pressures in an extreme way, as do families with husband and wife already in conflict over differing priorities. Even back in the 1940s, family therapists commented that Quaker parents seemed to suffer much more guilt over the manner in which they were carrying out their family responsibilities than did other parents. This would seem to be even more true today, as parents are caught in ever more extreme tensions between being present to the family and being present to the community.

While Quakers like to think of themselves as nonconformists, there is a special kind of Quaker conformity hinted at in the previous paragraph. There is an imaginary ideal Quaker somewhere, living out all the testimonies at every moment of every day. This ideal Quaker is a collective myth which Friends may use to put pressure on each other to conform to expectations that cannot be realistically met. Not only do adults feel this pressure, but as parents they put these pressures on their children. According to Fortunato Castillo,

> A conscientious pacifist couple with high standards may dutifully rear their children without being aware of the silent cruelty of the perfectionist drives. Instead of verbalizing feelings of anger, a silent, cold disapproval is felt by the growing children, compounded by their awareness of their smallness vis-à-vis the grown-

up, powerful parents. The aggressive drives of the children become greater by the inability to find expression.

Some adults who were raised as Quakers have bitter memories of being forced to share when there was no inward assent to the sharing. Each person has their own memories. Succumbing to Quaker conformity without developing the capacity for discernment and autonomous choice builds up the hidden residue of anger.

It can be argued that we have been too successful in creating appearances. David and Vera Mace, who first developed marriage enrichment retreats as a Quaker project and then moved to non-Quaker settings on the assumption that Quakers didn't need them, are now turning back to look at the Society of Friends in a state of shock. They have found that Friends need such programs as much or more than anyone else! The Maces, like many of us, have been deceived by appearances.

In spite of its nonconformist tradition, the Society of Friends can be hard on those who do not conform, who choose new ways to witness. I am thinking particularly of the storms caused by Friends who witness to personhood by declaring themselves lesbian or gay, and choose to publicly affirm new types of family relationships, new types of roles for men and women. This witness is usually based on strong inward leadings, and involves a kind of affirmation of equality, nonviolence, and community for which many Quakers in traditional gender-identified roles are not prepared. Are they perhaps new twentieth-century combatants in what George Fox called the "Lamb's War"?

Those who are concerned about Quaker overconformity usually come from meetings where there has been an active passing on of Quaker ways, traditions, and disciplines from generation to generation. There are many meetings in which this does not take place, whether because of a predominance of newly convinced Friends, or lack of energy and interest on the part of experienced Friends in the work of religious education. The result may be a tragic spiritual vacuum which leaves families floundering in the secular culture. One major concern today in many meetings is that too many convinced Friends have in fact not gone through the process of "convincement." They may have joined a group with whom they felt socially and politically comfortable without every having found out that this is supposed to involve trying to live in "that life and power that takes away the occasion of all wars". They may never have heard of Friends' queries, and if they have encountered the term "Quaker discipline," they may consider it quaint and old-fashioned, without relevance for today.

This is a very serious problem indeed. In terms of family life, it sets up a vicious cycle. Families that are not learning Quaker ways live out the secular culture in the midst of the meeting, thus quite unintentionally weakening by dilution the Quaker practices in families that do follow them. This further taxes the meeting's capacity to serve as teacher for new members.

What are Quaker family practices? They are varied; in fact, each family that takes its Quakerism seriously develops its own variant of Quaker culture. The uses of silence are important. Silence may be used to introduce all kinds of special occasions, from meals to family celebrations. Use of a listening dialogue at times of conflict and disagreement is another good family practice that is not necessarily unique to Quakers. Quaker values make themselves evident in the choice of books and other literature, in mass-media exposure, and in recreational patterns. In a very basic way, the level of household expenditures is, or should be, rooted in Quaker values. The ways in which families develop their Quaker culture provide the empirical answer to the question, "What does it mean to be a Quaker?" The responsibility of a meeting to introduce its new families to the meaning of Quaker culture, then, goes beyond its responsibility to new members. It is also a responsibility to keep strengthening and supporting the families already in membership.

Pressures toward secular values come from both within and without meeting communities. From within, the strains are associated with difficulties assimilating new members with little knowledge of Quaker disciplines. From without, Quakers feel the same role pressures that non-Quakers feel because the boundaries between the Quaker and the secular culture are increasingly permeable. There was a time when Quaker communities were largely separate from secular society, with their own schools and welfare institutions. Today, most of us have far more secular than Quaker influences in our daily lives. The occupational sphere, the mass media, and most of our sources of information about the world—all are secular.

One effect of this situation is that the testimony on equality between women and men, long considered a major feature of Quakerism both in family and public spheres, is daily eroded through non-Quaker sex-role socialization experiences from early childhood to old age. From attitudes in the neighborhood, classroom, community, and media, boys learn that to be men is to dominate, while girls learn that to be women is to be submissive. Many have deplored the gradual decline of leadership roles among women in the Society of Friends. Some attribute it to the discontinuance of separate men's and women's meetings. Others, such as Demie Kurz, see the erosion of the testimonies on equality and peace in Quaker families as part of the larger problem of increasing cultural emphasis on violence—again emphasizing the permeability and vulnerability of Quaker culture to the larger culture. She suggests that women are less affected than men by the new models of violence because sex role stereotypes call for nonviolence on the part of women.

Should we infer from this line of thought that the leadership Quaker women have given to the peace movement in recent years is simply a function of differential gender socialization with little additional impact from Quaker rearing? We can't answer this question because we know so little about the development of pacifism in individuals over the life span. Judy Brutz, who has done pioneering studies of violence in Quaker families, has taken a positive approach to an otherwise very painful problem. Instead of simply focusing on why violence occurs, she has asked how people become nonviolent. With this focus, it becomes possible to see the subtler influences of Quaker ways in shaping perceptions and behaviors over a wide range of situations during a lifetime.

By recording the oral histories of Friends of all ages, Brutz has found that understanding of the peace testimony, and ways of defining nonviolence and pacifism, change over the life span. From thinking in terms of specific behaviors, the pacifist approach broadens to include all areas of life, with increasing sensitivity to the many dimensions of violence in human experience. Most important of all, Brutz has found a gradual discovery over the lifetime of the interconnection between spiritual development and pacifism.

This corresponds very much to my own research, and to personal impressions gained over the years in trying to identify what the growing-up process is for peacemakers. For example, I found in my study of the women who became active in Women Strike for Peace in the early 1960s that while individuals may enter into public peace witness for the first time in middle age, there are usually early childhood events that triggered the process of growth. Receiving love and acceptance in early childhood, experiencing times of solitary reflection in puberty and adolescence, accepting early responsibility for self and others—this combination seems to produce peacemakers. Always we come back to what is happening in that most intimate setting of our lives, the household. Whether communal, single-parent, single-sex, nuclear, or multi-generational, the household is the space in which much of what we are is formed and re-formed over the life span. It is the physically present part of our family. Each of us has experienced many changes in the composition and characteristics of our household over the years, as family members come and go. The older we grow, the more varied our household experience. Still, it continues to form us.

If we call those who live in our household our immediate family, then we can say that the family is the practice space, the testing ground, for all our Quaker testimonies. Where else can we learn the difficult and sensitive process of mutual calibration between persistent differences which the Quaker testimony on equality calls for, if we don't try it at home? And if we don't work at that, what basis is there for abstaining from violence when things don't go our way? Demie Kurz sees a direct relationship between lack of practice of the testimony of equality and the presence of violence in Quaker families. Where there is acknowledged equality and respect for the other, there can be no violence.

It is the *developmental* character of pacifism, the fact that the peacemaker in us ripens slowly through a process of lifelong learning and discipline and prayer, that links the peace testimony so powerfully to the family. Everywhere else we are dealt with as segments of ourselves relevant to a given interaction. In the family we are willy-nilly whole. No part can be completely hidden, though we may try. The family may help or hinder our growth, but it is definitely a part of the process.

Does the family have a future? Asking this question has been a favorite parlor game inside and outside the Society of Friends for at least the past four decades. Once again the permeability of the boundary between Quaker and non-Quaker becomes evident, as women from both groups stream into the labor force. The question on both sides of that boundary is, who will look after the children? The concept of shared parenting and neighborhood child care as community responsibilities which can strengthen, not weaken, family life is still slow in developing. Nowhere is the Quaker testimony on equality more pertinent than in the case of shared parenting. It is a weak family that depends on a traditional gender-based division of labor to keep it going.

Divorce and remarriage rates have apparently stabilized after a period of rising marital dissolutions. Today, an important concern for the future is to help divorced families continue as support networks for one another after recombinations have occurred. The meeting community, with its clearness and Ministry and Counsel committees, will need to shift some of its attention away from the more dramatic struggles of marital dissolution, and toward the discipline of long-term involvement and support for members of recombined families. Here the testimony on community—that we are all part of one another—is again inseparable from the testimony on family life itself.

Economic hardship is frequently the aftermath of dissolutions, much more for women than for men. With the prospect of a continuing decline in the availability of well-paying jobs, many families will experience a decline in standard of living. The structure of the labor force is changing, and higher salaries will in the future be available chiefly to a professional and technological elite. What will it be like living in a society in which children cannot afford homes as large and comfortable as those their parents had? This is the time to remember that there have been longstanding complaints from Friends about the inroads of materialism and the consumer culture on family life. Is there an opportunity here to rethink within local meetings what the testimony on simplicity means?

Another looming problem area is the greatly lengthened life span. Children these days not only have living grandparents, they often have living great-grandparents. Treasured when there were few of them, grandparents are now being seen as a future burden to the economy, as the children, whose own economic expectations have already been lowered, face tax burdens and a staggering social security budget to support their long-lived elders. Already, we hear rhetoric about the war the young will be waging on the old.

What does the Society of Friends have to say to the larger community about this? At least Friends are getting ready to answer the question for themselves. Many meetings now have committees on aging, and new Friends retirement communities are being built at a rapid rate. But will this be only a physical-care approach? What about the social insight and spiritual wisdom that our elders have stored up over the decades? How will these treasures be drawn upon? If the rest of society is preparing for war on the

elderly, how do we prepare for their role as peacemakers—
and our own?

Once we start thinking in life-span terms, all important
social questions come to roost in the family.

Is there a way forward for the family, in spite of the
many problems that beset it? Can Quaker homes become
centers of peace and love, the colonies of heaven that Kenneth Boulding and I pictured when we married forty-five
years ago? Colonialism has a bad name in our time; yet
the kind of colony that is a center of peace and love for all
who enter is an outward-turning colony—an inclusive,
sharing community seeking ever-new bonds with the
larger human family. What are the signs of hope for this
kind of family?

First and foremost, there are many such families already
in our midst, and we should celebrate them, learn from
them. Exclusive attention to the problems and pains of
family life distracts us from appreciating the families who
manage those problems and pains and still have abundant
love and joy to share.

Second, we should appreciate the extent to which the
current focus on family problems, including family violence, is in fact the process of redrawing the contours of
our mental maps to reflect the bumpiness of family living
in this difficult age. No more whitewashing! The Quaker
researchers who have given us feedback on the extent of
family problems, and the therapists who are encouraging
an honest appraisal of the amount of attention and energy
required to productively handle our testimonies, our
stresses, and our high aspirations, are laying the
groundwork for an invigorated approach to family living.

Third, we have the experience of incorporating refugee
families into our meetings, going back to the 1930s when
meetings "adopted" refugee families from Europe. This
experience is taking on new dimensions as meetings not
only adopt refugee families from Central America, but offer

sanctuary, either literal or symbolic, as well. Sanctuary joins the issues of a just world order and just national policies with responsible community behavior, the spiritual vitality of the local Friends meeting, and family values. The courage and love these refugee families bring into our midst, as well as the problems, remind us once again how basic the family is in responding to catastrophe. These families are in themselves teachers for us.

Fourth, Friends have claimed space for a just world order in opposition to governmental policy by declaring the meetinghouse and the homes of meeting members nuclear free zones, or zones of peace. While this is a symbolic act, it also creates the opportunity for living in these zones of peace as if the Peaceable Commonwealth had already arrived.

Many more signs of the new seriousness with which family life is approached could be given. Instead, I will mention one more that is powerful because it knits together people whose individual family ties may have been shaken by death, divorce, a move, or reaching the empty-nest stage. I refer to the constructed extended family projects that many meetings have undertaken. Family-type groups are formed consisting of Friends of all ages, with anywhere from eight to twenty members. Meeting regularly, they share at many levels—from worship to recreation to deep discussion of personal and social issues. Sometimes they are simply called worship-sharing groups, but their special additional characteristic is that they include individuals of all ages and foster a closer bond between members than ordinary meeting activity can sustain.

What Can Meetings Do?

To balance out the problems and promises in this discussion of concerns for family life, I will close with some suggestions, made by the groups of Friends with whom I have held discussions, for strengthening the new trend of dealing more realistically with family problems.

1. Ministry and Oversight, or Ministry and Counsel, is the body within the Friends meeting charged with responsibility for the spiritual health of its members. Not infrequently, this body is unprepared to deal with the more severe family problems that exist within a meeting, particularly problems involving child and wife abuse. Sending members of these bodies to workshops dealing with such issues is one way of strengthening the ministry to families in a meeting. Making sure the composition of Ministry and Oversight committees reflects the range of spiritual and social wisdom in the meeting is another.

2. Meetings might consider forming intergenerational teams consisting of adolescents and the elderly for a variety of purposes. These two perspectives are too frequently excluded in dealing with meeting concerns as well as family concerns. Such task forces could bring recommendations to the meeting. They could do family visiting. They could be asked to serve as mediators in conflict situations. Drawing on both ends of the age spectrum will strengthen family life within meetings, as more acknowledgment and respect is given to contributions of the young and the old, and will also add to the vitality of the meeting itself.

3. Specific encouragement of family-to-family visiting within the meeting, perhaps even with sign-up sheets so that families not otherwise included can be involved, would enliven family interaction. Revival of the traditional practice of members visiting meeting families in their homes for worship-sharing and discussion might also be considered.

4. Meeting forums dealing with the application of Quaker testimonies in the home and larger community, jointly planned by junior and senior high First-Day school classes and members of the adult Religious Education Committee, would enable the adults of the meeting to see their children in a new light, and vice versa.

5. Making sure that all Quaker gatherings outside the local meeting have children as well as adults as appointed representatives will give another dimension to family participation in these gatherings.

6. Meetings can involve teenagers and adults in oral history projects with older members of the meeting, focusing particularly on their experiences as Quakers. There is so much to explore in an older person's memories!—childhood (whether Quaker or not), first contacts with Quakers, experiences in this and other meetings, personal searching, hard decisions, Quaker activities of an earlier time. An interpretation of the Quaker testimonies will emerge from these life stories which will be worth many hours of more formal discussion about Quaker beliefs. Putting the oral histories on tape—and, where feasible, in transcribed form as well—will help families in various stages of life appreciate the challenges and changes that lie ahead for them over the life span. Such a project might be combined with a study of selected Quaker journals kept by an earlier generation of Friends, with an encouragement to meeting members to start the practice of journal keeping as both individual and family projects.

Once a meeting starts thinking of projects that can bring the family aspect of its corporate life into clearer focus, there will be no lack of ideas, particularly when children are encouraged to participate in the process.

A few years ago I began personally living in what I call the two-hundred-year present. This means that today's present begins with the date of birth of those celebrating their hundredth birthday, and extends to the coming hundredth birthday of the babies born on this day. I can do this because my life is intertwined in so many ways with the lives of those born and to be born within that extended present moment, through all the human beings I have known and will know, inside and outside the family. These two hundred years are very much a part of the space in which I live and move. Sensing the immediacy of that time span makes the wisdom of those lives, the knowledge and experience accumulated and yet to come, more vividly accessible to me, and makes my sense of connectedness to the future as well as the past very strong.

I have from time to time shared this way of thinking and being and acting through my teaching and writing. I believe it gives us a new hold on the problems that beset us to realize that much of what we are struggling with now in the 1980s was also struggled with in the 1880s. Great insights have been gained and lost, creative new ways of managing human problems invented and ignored. Most important of all, families have lived out their lives through each successive time of turmoil. Children have dreamed dreams and have grown up to act them out as best they could. Today's future is being dreamed even now, for all the gloom and dread of the nuclear age. Much has been made of children's fears. Less attention is being paid to the other side of fear—children's hopes.

Wisdom, love, and joy have been nurtured in every age, along with ignorance, hatred, and envy. By living in the extended present, the wisdom, love, and joy become available to build on. The ignorance, hatred, and envy remain usefully visible to learn from. It is my hope and prayer for the Society of Friends that we can collectively live that two-hundred-year present. May every Friend be able to draw on the rich resources of human experience for building the next generation's world, in that setting which can nurture the best of what makes us human—our families.

Quaker Foremothers
as Ministers and Householders

The twenty-five women whose inward journeys are described here lived in times of turmoil not unlike our own, and drew on deep spiritual resources to meet the challenges of those times. They all had family responsibilities, were all active in the ministry (i.e., preaching and public service of various kinds), and were all considered saints by their meetings. English Quakers of the first five generations following the sect's founding, we know about them because their journals were published in a nineteenth-century compilation entitled *The Friends Library*.

These women lived under much stress, whether from persecutions, or a constant process of bereavement as children, spouses, relatives, and friends died around them. They had to struggle with their identity as women called to public spiritual leadership in a world unfriendly to Quaker practice, and in local meetings where many Friends, male and female, were lukewarm to the idea of women's leadership. Carrying heavy household responsibilities, they worked side by side with their husbands in field or shop, nursed the sick in a far-flung kin network, and ministered actively in their local meetings. They visited the sick, taught the children of the poor, oversaw the local workhouses, and visited nearby prisons and asylums. In addition, they were called to travel in the ministry, sometimes on trips that took them away from home for two or more years at a time. A deep and powerful prayer life sustained them, but they also engaged in unremitting spiritual struggles as to the rightness of their callings. They thought of themselves as channels of God's will, not social innovators. Nevertheless, the overflow from their prayer life helped create conditions for a spiritual and social regeneration of the society around them.

Of the twenty-five women, only ten had children. These ten nearly all had large families, however—seven to ten children. Nine remained childless in marriage, four marrying in or near their forties after they were already well known as ministers. Six remained single all their lives. Yet all had heavy household and nursing duties, as members of extended families. Some were of comfortable means like Margaret Fell and Elizabeth Fry; others were very poor, like Elizabeth Collins. Sent out to be a houseworker at the age of five when her father died, Elizabeth Collins was apprenticed at sixteen, married at eighteen, widowed at twenty-two with two children, and recorded as a minister of the Society at twenty-four. Other young women emigrated to America against their parents' will, worked their way out of indentured service under great hardship, and became ministers in the new land. Whether rich, poor, or of moderate means, they all worked hard and prayed long. They also lived considerably longer than their non-Quaker sisters of that era, with an average age at death of sixty-eight. Twelve lived into their eighties or nineties, five to their sixties, and five died at fifty or under. (For three no age at death is given.)

Having spent months immersed in their journals, I am struck by how severe the women appear in the following highly condensed account of certain aspects of their lives. The words they use to describe their struggle sound harsh, and their resolve not to be distracted by family duties has a steely character. In fact, all these women were spirited, complex individuals with a highly developed capacity to relate to others, and the Quaker circles they moved in had their own sober warmth and conviviality. The intensity of their calling to a public religious and social witness—and the barriers they had to leap over to respond to that calling—is what makes their words sound harsh. Furthermore, religious culture and the language in which it is expressed have changed a great deal in three centuries. As you read what these women say, imagine energetic, sensitive nonconformists engaged in a massive effort of spiritual transformation during an era of widespread violence and moral decay.

Spiritual Struggles in Youth

In the Society of Friends there are only queries, not specific practices, and all guidance comes from the Inward Teacher. Because there was no external authority to guide, discipline, and exhort them, these women disciplined themselves. Sometimes they saw themselves as spiritual children, needing to be nurtured and protected as "natural" children do, in a kind of probationary childhood, until ready for harder things. Sarah Grubb wrote of the need to accept the pace of her spiritual growth:

> I often wish that I could learn to be still when I have nothing to do, and instead of straining my eyes in the dark, and watching the breaking of the day, to dwell quietly in the ward all night, believing in the light, and obediently working therein. The outward day breaks gradually upon us, and experience teaches us the certain indication of its approach, a dawning of light which we are not apt to disbelieve, nor doubt that the meridian of it will come in due time. As in the outward, we cannot hasten that time, no more can we with respect to divine illuminations.

Few escaped a long period of struggle to adopt the higher code of conduct that the religious call demanded. Often the struggle centered on the use of the fateful words "thee" and "thou," which marked a person as clearly having chosen to be a Quaker. (Like the French *tu* and the German *du*, thee and thou were forms of address used for children and social inferiors. The Quaker testimony of equality led them to address everyone with this intimate form, which seemed rude to non-Quakers.) Elizabeth Stirredge recalled this period in her own life:

For my part, I had a concern upon my spirit, because I shifted many times from that word. I would have said any word, rather than thee or thou, that would have answered the matter I was concerned in, but still I was condemned, guilt following me. I was not clear in the sight of God; my way was hedged up with thorns; I could go no further, until I had yielded obedience unto the little things.

Elizabeth Fry wrote at age twenty, when she still loved worldly things:

How much my natural heart does love to sing: but if I give way to the ecstasy singing sometimes produces in my mind, it carries me far beyond the center; it increases all the world passions, and works on enthusiasm.

These women were practicing what Catholics would call "religious discernment." They were subjecting their thoughts, feelings, and impulses to criticism in the light of the divine knowledge available to them. Because they felt they were to be channels for communicating God's word to others, they judged themselves by the hardest standards they knew.

All the women struggled mightily against being called to the ministry. There were usually three crises. The first was in accepting an inward call to serious holiness. The second was accepting a call to speak in meeting. Some women struggled so hard against the inner call to speak that they became seriously ill, and the struggle could go on for several years. Spouses, children, relatives, an entire meeting could become involved in these struggles. Alice Hayes became seriously crippled and had to be cared for by her husband before she finally broke the bonds. Margaret Lucas longed and dreaded to go to meeting—longed for divine sustenance, dreaded the call to speak. Finally she managed. Overcoming "slavish fear," she got ready to kneel in vocal prayer:

While I viewed the place, my soul secretly breathed thus before the Lord, "Here is the place of my execution" . . . "This is the block whereon I must yield up the pride of nature, for a testimony of my obedience; remember me, O Lord! and the conflicts that I undergo to serve thee. Accept, O Lord! the sacrifice."

Yet there was still one more titanic struggle ahead, when the call came to travel in the ministry outside one's local meeting. Elizabeth Webb had a call to go to America. She became so ill while resisting it that when she finally gave in she had to be carried to shipboard on a litter. (This may not be precisely correct. The journal account is ambiguous, and she may have meant simply that she finally decided to go *even if* she had to be carried aboard on a litter.)

There were objective reasons for these struggles. They were not simply neurotic symptoms of an unbalanced emotional life. First, there was the problem of redefining one's role as a woman to fit the exacting demands of public ministry. Second, there was the rigorous training for the spiritual life and for the ministry that every woman must undergo who responded to the call. Lastly, there was the prospect of grueling hard work in traveling from meeting to meeting giving spiritual guidance. Travel in those times involved real physical risk: the dangers of shipwreck and of pirates and man o' wars at sea; the dangers of impassable roads and of brigands and thieves on land.

Not all spiritual calls involved traveling to faraway places, however. Sarah Stephenson was one of those who participated in creating a new type of ministry for the Society of Friends, a ministry to families in their homes. Before her innovation, ministry was confined to public meetings. She developed a way of "sitting" with families in their living rooms so that spiritual teaching could become individualized to the needs of even the youngest family member. For thirty-one years Sarah traveled throughout England visiting families; in the last sickness-ridden months of her life, she kept up a schedule of three family visits a day. Few could sustain such a pace and remain spiritually alive.

Family Life and Children

For insight into the family experiences of these Quaker women, today's women readers will have to draw heavily on imagination and extrapolation from their own experience. This is because actual references to family life are, with one or two notable exceptions, so reserved and sparse that it would be easy to conclude that these women were indifferent to their husbands and children. They were continually struggling with their "natural affections," just as they were struggling with their imaginations, and with their intellectual capacities—the Reasoner in them. Such struggles took place because they were more, not less, endowed with these faculties than other people. They imagined more, thought more, and loved more than most of their contemporaries.

However, even empathic reading of women's writings by women cannot overcome the gaps in understanding created by a sheer absence of references to certain types of basic human experience that belong in the realm of family life. We must draw on Elizabeth Fry for our only information on how these women faced childbirth, for example. She is the only one who even mentions, though very indirectly, the experience of being in labor. Having had a low pain threshold since childhood, each of her nine deliveries was a prolonged nightmare. I learned to recognize, in reading her journal, a certain somber tone that would creep into her entries in the months preceding each childbirth, and came to know just when to expect such terse lines as these: "Time runs on apace. I desire my imagination may not dwell on that which is before it. Every outward thing appears nearly, if not quite, ready; as for the inner preparation, I cannot prepare myself." (This a couple of weeks before delivery.) Three weeks after the birth: "A willing mind to suffer was hard to get at. I longed to have the cup removed from me." One line only on the day before the birth of her ninth child, when she was thirty-four: "Help, dearest Lord, or I perish." The rest she kept to herself, and so did all the other women who had nine, ten, or more babies. Childbirth was "natural," but for many, it was not without fear and pain. None of these women died in childbirth, but they had sisters who did.

The metaphor of the divine parent, the everlasting arms, is central to the spiritual life of these women. Why, then, are they so free to express their love for God, and so sparing in expressions of love for their own children? For us, the parent-child relationship and the experience of human birthing is so easily and naturally related to our experience of the divine parent and spiritual rebirth.

The word "naturally" is, I believe, the key to the difference. Quaker women ministers partook of a religious culture in which the religious call was a call to follow Christ, the inward presence and the outward example. This meant a commitment to the literal remaking of the human individual on the pattern of the divine. The religious call has always meant this, the saints taking it more literally than others. What was different in the religious culture of the centuries previous to our own was a strong sense of the sinfulness of the "natural being." Human nature was not in itself good. It had to be reborn as divine nature through cultivation of the Seed of God's Spirit within. The "oppression of the Seed" is a term the women used frequently in their journals. They saw the divine Seed, present in every human heart, being oppressed everywhere: among the world's people, among Friends, and in themselves. Their work was to liberate the Seed, and to do this they had to be ruthless with the "natural parts" of their own being and of others. The rooting out of self and self-will included rooting out both natural affections and natural reason. Only God's love and God's reason had room in the reborn person. Since rebirth was not a once-for-all process, but a lifelong struggle against ever-renewed oppression of the Seed by human causes, one could never be sure whether one's love was really a natural affection or whether it came from the divine source.

This uncertainty was precisely what these Quaker women struggled with, some more successfully than others. Since they all had their share of human imperfections, and a highly developed individuality which was threatened by the customary demands of motherhood (today we can say it as they could not), they were not all equally fond of their children at all times. Yet all of them took parenting with a high seriousness.

Ministers as Mothers

Jane Pearson was one of the women who struggled hardest with her motherhood. One of the most widely traveled of the ministers, she was also the most prone to sickness. She herself recognized this as related to the intensity of her struggle. (All the women were, in fact, very discerning about their illnesses, seeing them as symptoms of the struggle between their natural and higher selves.) Even as a grandmother, she was still struggling against affectionate feelings for her grandchildren and wrote on one occasion, when setting out to travel, about how hard it was to go. But she dared not "let the affectionate part take hold."

Elizabeth Stirredge was one of those who managed to integrate her natural and higher feelings for her children, but not without considerable struggle. Of the first generation of Friends, she and her husband were shopkeepers whose goods were repeatedly distrained in the routine persecution of Friends by the authorities. Her calls led her to testify before King Charles II about the persecution, and more than once the calls led her to prison. She fought hard against the call to testify before the king. Her children were young, and she could not believe she was to leave them:

> Thus did I reason and strive against it, till my sorrow was so great, that I knew not whether ever the Lord would accept of me again. Then I cried unto the Lord again and again, "Lord, if thou hast found me worthy, make my way plain before me, and I will follow thee; for thou knowest that I would not willingly offend thee." But knowing myself to be of a weak capacity, I did not think the

Lord would make choice of such a contemptible instrument as I, to leave my habitation and tender children, who were young, to go to King Charles, an hundred miles off, and with such a plain testimony as the Lord did require of me; which made me go bowed down many months under the exercise of it; and oftentimes strove against it. I could get no rest, but in giving up to obey the Lord in all things that he required of me; and though it seemed hard and strange to me, yet the Lord made hard things easy, according to his promise to me, when I was going from my children, and knew not but my life might be required for my testimony, it was so plain; and when I looked upon my children, my heart yearned towards them. These words ran through me, "If thou canst believe, thou shalt see all things accomplished, and thou shalt return in peace, and thy reward shall be with thee." . . .

So the Lord blessed my going forth, his presence was with me in my journey; preserved my family well, and my coming home was with joy and peace in my bosom.

At the age of fifty-seven, after one of the most eventful lives of any of these Quaker saints, she sat down to write her journal for her children and grandchildren. The journal tells us, both directly and indirectly, that she and her husband trained their children to be partners in the outward struggle and companions on the inward journey. Training the children was a theme often on the minds of the women:

The way you know; you have been trained up in it; and the concern of my spirit is, that you may keep in it, and be concerned for your children, as your father and I have been for you. Train them up in the way of truth, and keep them out of the beggarly rudiments of this world, that they may grow up in plainness; and keep to the plain language, both you and they; which is become a very indifferent thing amongst many of the professors of truth. But in the beginning we went through great exercise for that very word, thee and thou to one person.

The close of her journal is a beautiful prayer for her own children and God's flock everywhere, a powerful testimony to her own achievement in integrating human and divine love:

Strengthen my faith, hope and confidence, that I may steadfastly believe that thou wilt preserve my children, when I am gone to my resting place. . . . And now, I do wholly resign them into thy hands, knowing thou art able to keep them through faith, and to preserve them all their days, and to do more for them than I am able to ask of thee. Whatever exercise they meet with, strengthen them, and bear up their spirits, that they may not be overcome with the temptations of the wicked one: for, thy power hath been sufficient to redeem my soul. Lord, once more do I commit the keeping of my spirit to thee, with my children, and all thy flock and family upon the face of the earth, with whom my soul is at peace and in unity. I feel the renewings of thy love at this time, which is the greatest comfort that can be enjoyed; therefore does my heart, and all that is within me, return unto thee all praises, glory and honour, with hearty thanksgiving, and pure obedience for evermore.

Elizabeth Fry, who, as we have already seen, could write more freely of her natural being than others, gives us a glimpse of how the spiritual journey is shared with children in daily life. Family meeting for worship was part of the daily domestic rhythm, and the children witnessed the upward soarings of the parental spirit as well as the "dippedness of mind." One day after family meeting, Elizabeth wrote:

I had to pour forth a little of my soul; there appeared to flow a current of life and love, as if we were owned by the Most High; I felt my own like a song of praise. . . . I certainly was much raised spiritually.

Elizabeth worried a great deal about the effect on her children of her public ministry and work in prisons. She consulted with her brothers about this. Brother Joseph John Gurney reassured her that while the situation "is not what one would have chosen," it can do the children no harm to be exposed to concerns for the state of the world. Her children were as lively as she herself had been as a child, and she despaired of her inability to discipline them, but she loved them deeply. As adults they were friends and companions to her. The death of Elizabeth's five-year-old daughter Betsy gives one glimpse into a sadness that none of the mothers among these ministers escaped—the death of a child. Her journal entry shows her struggling with feelings of rebelliousness against committing the once vivacious little spirit to burial:

> Dearest Lord, be pleased to arise a little in thy own power, for the help of thy poor unworthy servant and handmaid; and if consistent with thy holy will, to dispel some of her distressing feelings, and make her willing to part with and commit to the earth her beloved child's body.

Mary Dudley had to struggle harder than most to integrate her parental and spiritual feelings, possibly because she had to struggle hard against her own parents as a young girl in leaving the family church to become a Friend. It had been necessary to overcome natural affection—considered synonymous with obedience to parental wishes—to answer the divine call. She went through the same conflict when her own children were born, since she had already been called to the ministry:

> Having a disposition naturally prone to affectionate attachment, I now began, in the addition of children, to feel my heart in danger of so centering in these gifts, as to fall short of occupying in the manner designed, with the gift received; and though at seasons I was brought in the secret of my heart to make an entire surrender to the work I saw that I was called to, yet when any little opening presented, how did I shrink from the demanded sacrifice, and crave to be excused in this thing; so that an enlargement was not witnessed for some years, though I several times took journeys, and experienced holy help to be extended.

Time and time again the call to the ministry won out over the calls of motherhood, but not easily:

> On returning to our lodgings found W.N., just come from Clonmel; he informed me that the young woman who had the chief care of my children had taken the measles, and was removed out of the house. I sensibly felt this intelligence, and the struggle was not small to endeavour after, and attain, a degree of quietude, sufficient to discover the right path.

> I went distressed to bed, I think honestly resigned, either to go forward or return home, as truth opened.

In fact, Mary continued her journey and was able to "dispense" thoughts of home. The hardest call came on the heels of the birth of her seventh child. Her journal editor writes that the youngest was "only ten weeks old, and her health was very delicate, so that the sacrifice was indeed great." Mary, however, reported a merciful extension of proportionate divine assistance for the journey undertaken.

One could argue that such behavior represented a rejection of parenthood and children, but the ongoing contact, letters, and expressions of mutual concern that continued until the death of each of these mothers argues against such simplistic explanations. Ruth Follows, an ardent logger of miles in the ministry and one whose journal reflects little but miles covered and number of meetings sat in, wrote letters to her children that reflect serious attempts at spiritual guidance:

[To her son Samuel]

Donnington, Eighth month 27th, 1779

—Go on patiently—Is it not good for thee to feel thy own burthen? Consider how much greater difficulty thousands are now in, who have large families, and very little to support them with.

I should be glad if I could say any thing that would be of service to thee, but thou well knowest that the best help is in thyself. O look there—ask of Him who "giveth liberally and upbraideth not." . . . O that my dear children may all overcome the wicked one, that so I may salute you as young men, who are strong, having the word of God abiding in you.

Patience Brayton kept to her ministry even while children (and husband) were dying of an unidentified illness at home, having begun a lively service at the age of twenty-one. Most of her travels were between the ages of thirty-eight and fifty-four. The year of the death of her husband

and two children was apparently too much for her "natural affections," and she remained home thenceforth until she died at sixty-one.

A letter to her daughter Hannah, written the year before the family deaths, shows how hard she was struggling. That she wished to be more and more given to the Lord's requirings "whether I ever see thee more or not" sounds hard and must be seen in the light of her later loss of heart for travel:

[To her daughter]

Namptwich, Old England
25th of Second Month, 1785

Dear child, Hannah Brayton,

I have had thee in my mind for many days, with fresh remembrance what a dutiful child thou hast been in the outward concerns of life. O my dear, I trust there is a blessing for thee in store, and I hope thou wilt labour for that blessing that fadeth not away; that the dew of heaven may rest upon thee in all thy undertakings; and if the Lord becomes thy director, thou wilt be directed aright, both in divine and outward things. I long to be more and more given up to the Lord's requirings, whether I ever see thee more or not; although thou feelest nearer to me than I can relate with pen, the favours of heaven I feel so near at times, surmount all other considerations; when that abates I long to see thee again, but I hope more and more to learn patience, in all my steppings along in this life, for I see the want of it more now than ever, in order to keep me low and humble; if I am exalted at any of these favours, then I shall be in great danger—I am ready to tremble, seeing the work so great. Oh, my child, though nature brings thee into my mind with nearness, yet believing there is one rich rewarder to them that hold out to the end. . . .

I remain thy affectionate mother,
Patience Brayton

We see in the struggles of these women with their parenting role a foreshadow of the struggles of today's women. The overarching concept of a divine love that could transform and encompass the natural affections was ever-present as both a goad to the struggle and a solution to it. We shall see shortly how the resolutions of these struggles came about in the last years of the aging Quaker saints.

Husbands and Friends

The Quaker testimony on equality in all human relationships takes on particular importance when applied to husband-wife relationships. It has consistently been one of the strengths of the Society of Friends that when women and men marry, they take each other "with divine assistance," each promising to be to the other a loving and faithful spouse. Obedience is to God only, not to the husband. The patriarchal concept of wifely obedience which distorts the marriage covenant in the mainstream Christian tradition has no place in the Quaker marriage.

Partnership in obedience to God, however, was not easily arrived at in an era that had firm expectations concerning the submission of women. At least one of the women was physically abused by her non-Quaker husband when she joined the Society of Friends after their marriage. This was Elizabeth Ashbridge, the intrepid adventurer who arrived in America in her teens as an indentured servant. True to the expectations of both secular and Quaker society, she endured uncomplainingly and won him over in the end. Alice Hayes, one of the first-generation Quaker women ministers, was punished by her farmer husband for going to meeting. He relented some years later. When both husband and wife were Quaker, however, there was strong meeting support for a woman minister once she had been recognized and recorded. Husbands who were unenthusiastic about their wives' ministry generally kept quiet about it. Those men who were outspoken against women in the ministry, like John Story, evidently had stay-at-home wives.

The affection of Quaker husbands and wives for one another was frequently commented on by non-Quaker writers. Thomas Clarkson's statement in *Portraiture of*

Quakerism that connubial bliss was the chief recreation of Friends has often been quoted. Nevertheless, when the divine call to the ministry came, women had the same struggle with their natural affections in regard to their husbands that they had with their children. Sarah Grubb, whose public ministry began at age twenty-four, was much concerned about the danger of "settling down in outward enjoyments" when she married two years later. In fact, she took off on a major religious visitation to Scotland with a woman Friend just two weeks after her marriage, and was rarely home as much as a month at a time afterwards. She had no children, not surprisingly, and died the youngest of all these ministers, at the age of thirty-five. Here are her thoughts on marriage and the spiritual life, toward the end of her life, in a letter to a friend:

> Twelfth month 1789—I have seen, in my short life, so much fallacy in human wisdom respecting matrimonial connections, and so much blessing showered upon an attention to simple uncorrupted openings, which have not at first appeared most plausible, that I seem to have no faith left in any direction but that which the devoted heart finds to make for peace. In concerns of this sort, it is often very difficult for such to judge, because prepossession and inclination are apt to influence our best feelings. Natural affection bears some resemblance to sacred impulse; and therefore, methinks that this seed, though ever so right, must die in the ground before it be quickened and sanctified. In short there are few openings, for our own and the general good, which have not to pass through this temporary death, few gifts but what are designed to be buried in baptism; and I wish thee, if ever thou possess a female companion, to obtain her as a fruit of the new creation; that so thou mayest reap those spiritual advantages which those enjoy, who, through the effectual working of the grace of God, drink together into one spirit, whether in suffering or in rejoicing; for without this experience, Zion's travellers must find such connections to be secretly burthensome and insipid.

Her perceptive recognition that "natural affection bears some resemblance to sacred impulse" both goes to the heart of the conflict as these women experienced it, and points to its resolution.

Elizabeth Webb is the Friend who fell ill in struggling

against her call to go to America. Her husband bore the full brunt of the struggle, and belongs to the ranks of the unsung husbands of saints:

> I then told my husband that I had a concern to go to America; and asked him if he could give me up. He said he hoped it would not be required of me; but I told him it was; and that I should not go without his free consent, which seemed a little hard to him at first. A little while after, I was taken with a violent fever, which brought me so weak, that all who saw me thought I should not recover. But I thought my day's work was not done, and my chief concern in my sickness was about going to America. Some were troubled that I had made it public, because they thought I should die, and people would speak reproachfully of me; and said, if I did recover, the ship would be ready to sail before I should be fit to go, etc. But I thought if they would only carry me and lay me down in the ship, I should be well: for the Lord was very gracious to my soul in the time of my sickness, and gave me a promise that his presence should go with me. And then my husband was made very willing to give me up; he said, if it were for seven years, rather than to have me taken from him for ever.

Catharine Phillips had no such struggle. Her journal is almost a love song to her husband. She married late in life, and they had only thirteen years together. There is no shadow of conflict between the divine and human love:

> The tie of natural affection betwixt us was strong, arising from a similarity of sentiments, which was strengthened by an infinitely higher connection.

In another passage she emphasized the complementarity of her ministry and their partnership:

> An affectionately tender husband—ah, me! how shall I delineate this part of his character! Bound to me by the endearing ties of love and friendship, heightened by religious sympathy, his respect as well as affection, was apparent to our friends and acquaintance. His abilities to assist me in my religious engagements were conspicuous; for although he had no share in the ministerial labour, he was ready to promote it.

She remarked elsewhere that their tie was "superior to nature, though nature had a share in it."

Anne Camm was even more lyrical about the divine-human nature of the spousal tie. After the death of her first husband she wrote:

> And by the quickening of his holy power, we were made one in a spiritual and heavenly relation—our hearts being knit together in the unspeakable love of God, which was our joy and delight, and made our days together exceedingly comfortable—our temporal enjoyments being sanctified by it, and made a blessing to us. How hard it was, and how great a loss to me, to part with so dear and tender a husband, is far beyond what I can express. My tongue or pen is not able to set forth my sorrow.

Anne Camm twice had the good fortune to marry a fellow minister, and they worked and traveled both separately and together. If we wonder how such a husband-wife team appears from the point of view of the husband, here is the record of John Bell about his partnership with his deceased wife Deborah:

> She was a loving and affectionate wife, and the gift of God to me, and as such I always prized her, a help-meet indeed both in prosperity and adversity, a steady and cheerful companion in all the afflictions and trials which attended us, and a true and faithful yoke-fellow in all our services in the church; for being ever one in spirit, we became one in faith and practice, in discerning and judgment, and our concern and labour was the same; which nearly united us, and a life of comfort and satisfaction we lived, our souls in the nearest union delighting in each other; and the love and presence of God, wherewith we were often favoured in our private retirements, sweetened every bitter cup, and made our passage easy and pleasant to us.

It happens that Phillips, Camm, and Bell all had childless marriages. Undoubtedly it was easier to develop this tender dual-nature relationship (i.e., having both a sacred and everyday dimension) when there were no children present. While the practice of recognizing women ministers implies equality, in fact the primary feeling of responsibility for children fell more heavily on the mother than the father. The stress created by this asymmetry may well have inhibited the dual-nature bonding between parents that the childless couples apparently experienced without effort. Each woman sought her own unique balance of the "natural" and the "spiritual" in marriage. None failed completely to achieve some kind of balance, but some found it more easily than others.

Friendships between women, and sometimes between men and women outside of marriage, could assume the same profoundly tender divine-human character as spousal relationships. Many of the journal records are really letters to friends, lovingly preserved by the other party and incorporated into the memoirs of the deceased. Here is Quaker equality in one of its purest forms. Friends gave spiritual guidance to one another, lent the spiritual ear to one another, gave wholehearted, undemanding support to one another. Letters to friends can be as lyrical as those to spouses:

> Eighth month, 1789—Thou art, dear friend, an epistle written in my heart, where I sometimes read thee and thy mournful, humble steppings, with joy; consistent with the divine command to rejoice in his new creation, of which, in infinite mercy, thou art happily a part.

The Last of Life, and the First

Intimations of an unseen presence come very early to children. This apparent sensitivity to spiritual reality can be heightened by early and frequent experiences of death— death of adults, death of other children. All the women of our group had vivid recollections from early childhood of a sense of divine presence. They also vividly recall their fear of estrangement and separation from God and from their families, of being called too soon by the Angel of Death. Sin was a familiar concept at an early age, and they felt answerable for the sin of disobedience long before they

developed the inner disciplines of obedience. Salvation
and damnation are themes they were made aware of as
soon as they could talk, and they wondered anxiously
when other children died whether they had been saved
or damned.

In childhood these women also exhibited unusual liveliness of spirit and a capacity for sheer enjoyment of living.
This liveliness of spirit and concern about death combined
to set the stage for the titanic spiritual struggle they went
through as teenagers and on into their early twenties, when
they felt the inward call to holiness. The tension was all
the stronger because they felt that what was required of
them was possible, even if so many of their inclinations
went the other way. Moments of great spiritual peace and
joy alternated with despair, and they felt that the choice
between salvation and damnation was really theirs. Once
the battle was won and the call to the ministry answered,
the fear of damnation disappeared, but the struggle for
more perfect obedience went on.

I have emphasized that the struggle to be a perfect instrument of God's will continued over the years. The continual
doing of God's will did not save the saint from anguish
and despondency. What was done could never be enough.
It is the lot of the saint always to demand far more of the
self than ordinary people, so from one point of view these
women were struggling throughout life for ever higher
levels of goodness, toward ever more perfect obedience.
Yet the "dippedness of mind" that attacked them also had
a childlike quality. Can it be that the saint has a very
prolonged spiritual childhood?

The spiritual childhood appears to come to an end, finally, in the last years. The everlasting arms hold the aging
saint more steadily. There is a great sense of being near
home, of mission accomplished, of greater tolerance of the
human condition. There is also a wonderful sense of new
spiritual growth, of new understandings, new experiences
of God's love. Friends were very aware of this surge of
spiritual wisdom and strength in their elder saints, and
were careful to record their utterances when the saints

were too feeble to write themselves. Family and friends would gather about in the final days; one sometimes gets the impression that the bedrooms of the dying were rather crowded. If the dying took a long time—sometimes it went on for months—the crowds came, went, and came again. Deathbed utterances were particularly prized as glimpses of the glory ahead for those left behind.

This emphasis on spiritual illumination from the dying is the more extraordinary when one realizes that most of them were suffering severe physical pain in their final months, and particularly in their final days and hours. They knew what was expected of them by others. More important, they knew what they expected of themselves. Sometimes they feared they may not be up to the final trial of pain on the path to glory, and prayed for endurance. Mary Dudley was reported to have spoken in this manner:

> Afterwards, when under considerable suffering of body, she prayed for patience, and added, "Oh! if I should become impatient with the divine will, what reproach it would occasion. I feel poor and empty, and when lying awake am not able to fix my thoughts upon what I desire and prefer, but little things present, and this tries me. David speaks of having songs in the night, but I sometimes say, these, meaning intrusive thoughts, are not the Lord's songs."
>
> Several times when taking leave of her family for the night, she solemnly uttered this short petition, "Gracious Lord prepare us for what is to come." And when suffering from pain, and the feeling of general irritation, she frequently petitioned, "Lord enable us to trust that thou wilt never lay more on me than thou wilt give strength and patience to endure," adding, "Pray that I may have patience."

The initial shift from a life of great physical activity to a life limited by physical incapacity can be a trying one. We can follow the progression in Jane Pearson from her first exclamation, "I dread being at ease in Zion!" toward contentment: "The older and more infirm I grow the more I am enlarged in mind." At seventy-five, reading her old journals, she "feels a renewing of ancient power." She continued to prepare spiritually for her great transition:

Previous to this precious season, I had had very great openings into Divine things, pertaining to another life; things so sacred as not to be meddled with; which brought me to think I should soon be gathered.

At age seventy-eight, the transition was still in process:

Although I am exceedingly shaken, and my hand very unsteady, yet if it is right for me to leave to posterity, the memorable condescension of the Almighty to me, a poor worm, I shall be able to make it legible. Upon the 13th of twelfth month, 1813, sitting in the evening by my fire-side, with company about me engaged in conversing, I felt a strong attraction heavenward, which I was glad to feel: and a gracious God seemed pleased to bow his heavens and come down, directing me to dismiss every doubt respecting my own exit; for that he would take me in his mercy, and support me through what might befall me; and my charge was, never more to doubt of my eternal rest.

At age seventy-nine, we find the last journal entry in her own hand:

Ninth month 19th, 1814—This morning I again had the most strengthening, consoling evidence of Divine favour, that my poor frame could bear; letting me know that as my strength decreased, his watchful care over me increased; and although he had seen meet nearly to deprive me of my outward hearing, he had increased the inward so surprisingly, that I often seem to fall down before him in astonishment; my mind being so expanded and enlarged, that as naturals abate, spirituals increase; and my dear Redeemer allows me at seasons, to repose as upon his bosom.

The journey was accomplished. God touched each of these women in their very early years, and returned as a beloved companion to guide them through the gates of death. In all the decades in between there was an alternation of struggle and tranquility, of stormy clouds and radiant light. In the course of the journey, they carried their families with them, metaphorically or literally reshaped the world around them, and themselves became transformed.

The language of experience has changed from their day to ours, but the journey remains the same.

Quaker Women Included in This Essay

Elizabeth Ashbridge	1713-1755
Deborah Bell	1689-1738
Patience Brayton	1733-1794
Anne Camm	1627-1705
Elizabeth Collins	1755-1831
Mary Dudley	1750-1820
Ruth Follows	1718-1809
Margaret Fell	1614-1702
Elizabeth Fry	1780-1845
Sarah Grubb	1756-1791
Alice Hayes	1657-1720
Margaret Lucas	1701-1769
Jane Pearson	1735-1816
Catharine Phillips	1726-1794
Sarah Stephenson	1738-1802
Elizabeth Stirredge	1634-1706
Elizabeth Webb	no dates; journal letter written in 1712

The Challenge of Nonconformity: Reweaving the Web of Family Life for Gays and Lesbians

Reweaving webs of relationship is our main business in life. The process begins with the great separation that is birth. The ensuing bonding/reweaving between parents and newborn child is no simple process because the individuality and conflicting needs of each assert themselves almost at once. All through life we go on bonding across differences, because we need others to make us whole. The tension involved in that bonding is part of the human condition, and we ignore or underestimate it at our peril. Loving isn't easy.

Those who are called to nonconforming witnesses have a particularly complex task in reweaving relationships because there are more differences to bond across. We know that many family webs were ruptured in wartime because families could not support sons who chose conscientious objection or nonregistration. A special witness of nonconformity is the gay and lesbian act of "coming out." This involves publicly affirming the spiritual, social, and biological rightness of forming a primary bond with a person of one's own sex—women loving women (lesbians) and men loving men (gays). It also means witnessing to the wholeness of each human being, man and woman. "There is neither Jew nor Greek, there is neither slave nor free, there is neither male nor female; for you all are one in Christ Jesus" *(Galatians 3:28).*

This witness to oneness is something all of us can share with lesbians and gays, at the same time acknowledging that primary bonding with a person of one's own sex is a special case of the sexual bonding of the species. Some heterosexuals unite so strongly with the gay witness for wholeness and against the gender distinctions that warp personhood that they declare themselves "spiritual gays." (For the sake of simplicity I will use the term gay to refer to both lesbians and gays in this essay.) That fellowship of concern is important to gays because their nonconformity results in the breaking of many family and community bonds as family and friends reject the nonconforming position. The rejection causes pain and anguish heightened by a public unwillingness to acknowledge even the legitimacy of the pain, let alone the position taken.

It is important for Friends to understand the consequences for those in their midst who make the nonconforming choice of being publicly gay. Because recent decades have been a relatively easy time for Friends—a time of respectability—many have forgotten or never knew the pain of nonconformity. Yet many of us who were rearing children at the close of World War II spent much time thinking about how to rear them to be war-rejecting nonconformists. The post-Hiroshima world looked very bleak indeed. It was not something we wanted our children to be part of. We wanted them to help shape and be citizens of a very different world.

In those years I read about the lives of many peace-committed social-change activists, hoping to find some clues to what gave them strength for nonconformity. I found certain common elements in the childhood of each: (1) an experience of solitude and separation from society in childhood, whether through illness, isolated living, family differentness, or other reasons; (2) an experience of close attachment to some adult while young, inside or outside the family; and (3) a capacity to daydream, to envision a different and better world, which became the basis for reconnecting with society-as-it-could-be. The combination of having experienced both separation and bonding seemed to make the vision of the other possible, and drew the nonconforming activist to the work of reweaving the social web on behalf of the vision. Many Quaker gays and lesbians fit that model of social change activists.

Today the Quaker gay community has a special calling to reweave the social web on behalf of gays' vision. Their nonconforming witness comes out of the pain of their isolation, from the strength of the love they have known, and from the image of a different future social order. Many Friends are not only unaware of the social nature of the gay witness, they are unaware that it is a witness at all. The gays' nonconforming position is all too often seen only in terms of human rights. In fact the gay position represents a deepening and enriching of Quaker testimonies on equality, nonviolence, community, and simplicity, and as such deserves our respect, love, and support.

Let us look at the gay contribution to the Quaker testimonies:

Equality

The gay position goes beyond generally affirming equality in human relations. It deals with the specifics of the subordination of women to men, and with the specifics of all subordination—women to women and men to men. It sees inequality with X-ray eyes, in relation to age, class, ethnic, or cultural differences. Most of us affirm the testimony to equality without doing anything very complicated to maintain it. Gayness, however, sets aside all the conventional signs and symbols associated with traditional gender-based roles—which are also signs and symbols of inequality—and calls for crafting relationships that fully acknowledge the other as equal. Nothing can be taken for granted. It is only when one looks at society through gay eyes that one realizes how much unthinking social subordination goes on in daily life. Yes, much of it is "harmless," but it is all part of the web of inequality. Early Friends took objection to hat honor and the honorific "you" with the same seriousness that gays take objection to gender and status honoring.

Community

The gay witness to community permits no gender barriers to assumption of responsibility. On the other hand, it gives a new positive definition to age-old customs in every society of women gathering with women and men gathering with men in various settings and for various occasions. The community of women helping women has been a positive nurturing force in society, and so has the community of men helping men (when the latter has not involved warmaking). At present we move bumpily between same-sex and heterosexual groupings in our social enterprises. Gays can help enrich our understanding of the potentialities and strengths of each type of grouping.

Simplicity

What many gays bring to the witness of simplicity is not only a rejection of material accumulation for its own sake, but a highly developed aesthetic sense for the patterning of our environment. Whether the general public knows it or not, gays have made tremendous contributions to our society in the arts and humanities, and the tradition of doing so goes back a long way. Quaker "plain" turns beautiful.

Celebration

Another contribution of gayness which infuriates many is the gay gift for celebration, for joyfulness, for the dance of life. A gay dance is a very different affair from most public dances, open and welcoming to all ages in the best tradition of Quaker family dancing—a needed counterweight to the Quaker tendency to gloom. Behind the gay joyfulness, won at great cost, is the deep spiritual experience of accepting one's own gay identity, of being able to say aloud and in public, with pride and with grace, "I am gay."

Discipline

Finally, there is the witness of the disciplined life. Discipline is a hard word to understand. By "disciplined life" I mean a careful intentionality, a choosing, a discerning, in all one's actions. Gays who choose the responsibility of being publicly gay set aside conventional social role assignments, and thus subject themselves to a constant process of discernment. Life has to be organized and directed toward the living of a new wholeness, to the crafting of a new person.

Reweaving the web at the family level is where broken bonds are most painful. Quaker gays have parents, grandparents, brothers, sisters, cousins, aunts, and uncles like everyone else, but they are often (not always) treated as black sheep. When they form couples and marry, they would often like to be married under the care of their local meeting, but find it difficult to communicate that wish. They sometimes have children from former marriages, sometimes adopt children, sometimes take in singles with children—and very often serve in the time-honored role of extra parenting adult. Many of them work with children as teachers and caregivers. Like the celibate Shakers of an earlier era, many gays love children and take care that there are children in their lives.

What is a family? In the broadest sense it is a complex of households of relatives spread widely over one or more continents, some of which carry out the functions of reproduction. In theory these households keep in touch and care about one another; from time to time they meet for family reunions. Sometimes gays are invited to family reunions, sometimes not. Most households develop an additional "extended family" of friends who are "like one of the family." Such extended families are especially important to gays. Sometimes Friends meetings organize extended family groups as part of the ministry of the meeting community, and gays are often part of these.

The sad truth, however, is that gays usually find themselves outside the family networks they most value, cut off from people they love, by the social obsession that gays are unnatural, pathological people. The strengths that gays have to offer their families are so many, the rewards for their families of experiencing reconnection so great, one can only hope that families will increasingly reconsider mending ruptured relationships with gay offspring.

Many gays have special gifts and insights regarding family relationships which can strengthen both their families of origin and meeting families. These parallel the testimonies mentioned earlier. First and foremost is the testimony to equality in couple relationships. Because they accept no gender-based status differentials, gay couples are challenged with crafting an equality of relationship that few heterosexual partnerships achieve. Needless to say, it is based on a continuing openness to each other. At the same time, however, it must be remembered that gay couples live under stress. Gay couples long for stability and long-term relationships, but occasionally experience the same painful marital dissolutions that heterosexual couples go through.

They are denied the buffering effect that extended families provide young couples when troubles arise. The longing to reweave the family web and feel the support of parents and extended biological family is one of the most poignant aspects of being gay. The longing to reweave the web is not only personal; it is social. Gays long to help shape a society in which human beings and families are more gentle with one another.

How can the family web be rewoven? Caring about one's family does not in itself bring about reconnection, or there would be few gays separated from their families, so a kind of negotiation would seem in order. When differences are strong, mutual respect is the scarcest resource. In the case of gays, parents often do not respect their gayness, and gays themselves begin (sometimes unconsciously) to lose respect for their parents' continuing inability to accept their sons and daughters in new identities. For gays to work on ways to let their families know they respect them may be an important part of the process of winning respect in return.

Negotiation requires discovering common interests. One strong common interest between gays and their families is the hidden love on both sides which longs to find expression. It can be drawn out with patience. Negotiation also requires a willingness to "give" on matters of lesser concern. What can gays "give" on? What can their families "give" on?

The strength for gays to try reweaving the broken web comes from the support of friends. Can Quaker meetings be friends to gays, and support them in their efforts to reconnect with their families? That kind of support implies a recognition of the gay identity of the gay single or gay couple in the meeting. It means a willingness to share their other burdens as well, and an appreciation of what they bring to the meeting. It means gays taking committee and clerking responsibilities in the meeting. For some meetings, marriage of the gay couple under the care of the meeting has been an occasion of great spiritual deepening.

Quaker gays are *Quaker*. Gays active in any community of faith are likely to enrich that faith in similar ways. Quaker gays witness to the Quaker way of life, and bring special strengths to that witness in their manner of practicing equality, nonviolence, community, celebration, and discipline. The gay identity is itself part of that witness, striving for wholeness and oneness in the spirit of the teachings of Jesus. The witness should be honored.

Never in history has the Society of Friends needed more imagination and wisdom in demonstrating the possibility of living in "that life and spirit that takes away the occasion of all wars." Learning new ways of approaching gender identity, and new ways for men and women to live and work separately and together in building the Peaceable Commonwealth, is urgent for us all. The gays and lesbians among us can help us in our learning and in our doing. It is time for them to be freed from the stereotype of embattled victims fighting for the right to be what they are, and instead be accepted as coworkers in reweaving the social web for us all.

Family and Society

The Family as a Practice Ground
in Making History

During my years as a college professor with a number
of national and international committee and task force assignments, I increasingly came to feel the relevance of my
previous twenty-five year apprenticeship in homemaking
and community activism. What follows are some reflections on the meaning of that apprenticeship.

When we talk of "making history," we often think of
dramatic public acts. Yet, history is really made by the
painstaking accumulation of different kinds of experiences
and skills in private and public settings. We can never
really act "on the national scene" or "on the international
scene." We can only act in specific geographical and social
spaces which may serve as metaphors for larger scenes. It
is our *intending the metaphor* that gives our actions significance. Work done on tax legislation in a local branch of
the League of Women Voters is as much national as similar
work done in Washington D.C., which is, after all, only
another locality. Work done on disarmament measures in
a local branch of the Women's International League for
Peace and Freedom is as much international as similar
work done in the United Nations buildings in New York
or Geneva, which are also only other localities. One of the
frightening things about professors, planners, policy makers, and politicians is that the metaphors often seem more
real to them than the specific underlying human experience. Tools and technologies can insulate those who use
them from the reality they are supposed to be working on,

so that in the end they may live in a strange dream world of unlimited energy sources, unlimited military power, and unlimited world-spanning administrative capabilities.

I often find myself sitting in these insulated, unreal worlds. In order to stay in touch with human reality, particularly when discussions get inappropriately theoretical and off the track, I reach back in my mind for specific situational grounding in past experience. Administrative jurisdictional squabbles have been illuminated by recollections of how our children, sharing play space in any always-too-small room, used to erect barriers when the tension rose, to delineate their turf. Memories of my backyard disarmament campaign among the children of Bedford Road in Ann Arbor have facilitated analyses of the SALT talks.

What learnings from the family years are most important to me now? They came largely in the context of Quaker community and particularly a community of women and children. An extended family of about half a dozen young Ann Arbor Friends Meeting couples, all having four or five children close together in the late 1940s and early 1950s, was the setting in which we carried out many of our family activities, even to the extent of sharing bed and board with each others' children for sometimes short, sometimes long periods. On weekends we potlucked, camped, and worked on meeting projects—with all ages together on everything. On weekdays it was the women and the children. We recreated together and we did community action together—sometimes in WILPF or Fellowship of Reconciliation, sometimes in PTA or the local democratic party, sometimes in an explicitly Quaker group. Friends Lake Community, eighty acres on a small lake near Chelsea purchased by several dozen Quaker and non-Quaker families of Ann Arbor and nearby meetings, provided a setting which minimized the age and sex boundaries that were inevitable in the more segregated society of those times. There, no one was ever out of place, no matter what they did. Around the campfire at the edge of the lake we sang the songs and dreamed the revolutions that permeated every other part of our lives in the workaday world. Friends Lake was no accident. It was searched for, designed, planned, and created as a nurturing ground for our dreams—and for our children's dreams.

Particularly among the mothers, the single most important and recurring theme in all our dreamer-discussions was, "What will lead our children to grow up peacemakers?" The majority of the young fathers in the meeting had served in civilian public service camps as conscientious objectors in World War II. Would our children choose the nonviolent path? The larger community, outside the Friends meeting, was very far from peaceful in its attitudes. The query, "Would our children choose the nonviolent path in their own lives?" became the touchstone by which we judged all our actions, our lifestyle, everything. We were very conscientious (or thought we were) about leaving room for our children to choose their own way, but we wanted there to be good ways open before them. We women hardly ever did adults-only activities, except in the evening after the children had gone to bed. When we gathered at the county courthouse for the first Women's Strike for Peace; when we vigiled at the Pentagon or at Fort Dietrich or under the campus flagpole; when we marched in silent processions through town, the children were with us. When we organized literature displays, made posters, planned strategies, prepared mailings, cooked potlucks—even when we had our study meetings, the children were with us. When we went on work camps, the children were with us. They shared our tasks and also wove their play around our activities. All of us parents were totally involved in the First-Day school, as well as in the promotion of every kind of learning experience for our children.

One couple from our group went on to write a book with their eldest son, now a professor of sociology, on the biographies and childhood experiences of persons who have become eminent as adults in this century. I could hear Mildred Goertzel's voice from our long-ago times together as I read *33 Eminent Personalities*. The book concludes that a high degree of parental involvement in the learning experiences of children is the one thing most strongly associated with becoming a creative person as an adult. Mildred, like each woman in that group, has found a way in her post-childrearing professional life to work further on our old burning question of how to produce peacemakers. Her findings, confirmed in my own research on socialization for nonviolence, and in the work of all the other women of our once-upon-a-time extended family, have also been confirmed in the creative lives of our children. As young adults they have taken a great variety of paths, sometimes very difficult ones, and they are all in one way or another shapers and reconstructors of the world they live in.

The world of child-adult camaraderie we inhabited was fun, and it was challenging. Actually, my first experience in research and writing was in the preparation of a First-Day school pamphlet entitled "My Part in the Quaker Adventure." That pamphlet also happened to utilize holistic family involvement in education—the learning pattern we were all following. The teacher-student dialogues of Sunday mornings are among my favorite memories of those years, and if the children remember them far less vividly than I do, that is appropriate enough. I was learning more from them than they were from me. I hope the respect and appreciation I gave them was some small contribution to their well-being. Many Sundays I would come home from meeting in a state of combined spiritual exaltation and high intellectual excitement, because the children had said such remarkable things during class.

Three vivid impressions stand out from those years: the sense of being surrounded by and taught by children; the silent thankfulness of coming into meeting for worship as a family group (a memory interwoven with the hand-holding silences before meals at home); and the joyful solemnity of the various occasions when we stood or walked side by side with our children in public witness.

The sense of partnership with children and young people in world-building, which has been so strong with me all my adult life, unfortunately faces a trend in the opposite direction today. Research reports coming in from all directions state that parents are spending less time with their children than formerly and are less involved with their learning. Adults generally see and interact less with children than they did three decades ago. The International Year of the Child (1978) did not really address this problem. Adults met to talk about children and how they could be "protected," and largely avoided direct dialogue with young persons. I wrote *Children's Rights and the Wheel of Life* for the Year of the Child in hopes of introducing fresh perceptions about a world-building partnership of young, middle year, and elderly folk. It will take time for these perceptions to bear fruit.

As I look at my professional involvements, I see them all as direct extensions of earlier home and community-based activities. As a researcher building models of a peaceful world order and looking at trust-generating processes, institutions, and social roles, I am doing at another level what I did as a homemaker in Ann Arbor many years ago. Serving on the Council of the United Nations University or the UNESCO Peace Prize Jury or the Commission to Establish a United States Academy of Peace are all variants of my early PTA and neighborhood association experiences. And having learned to listen to children has made it much easier to engage in a listening kind of teaching with college students. Because I am always aware of local-global connections myself wherever I am and whatever I am doing, I try to share that sense of connectedness in whatever setting I find myself.

If we are to have more realistic and viable planning for world order, more people must see the connections between the family, the local habitat, and the international sphere. Men often have more trouble seeing those connections than women do. That is why increased involvement of men in family life and child nurture is crucial for the development of their peacemaking capabilities. When fathers spend as much time with children as mothers, false macho images of adult power and dominance can be tested against the flexible and ever-changing reality of the playground, to the great benefit of policy makers. The men's awareness movement and the gay and lesbians concern movement, both inside and outside the Society of Friends, play important roles in this process of developing new peacemaking capabilities. So does the children's movement, which has to be re-created by each new cohort of children.

Women often reject their own experience and social perceptions of family-world connectedness, because these experiences are associated with feeling oppressed and excluded. However, the interconnectedness of the local and the global has to be redefined, or we will all—women and men alike—get further and further away from the kind of world-building that is grounded in the human possibility. I have never found a better touchstone for evaluating my activities than the old question of my homemaking days: "Will this help the children grow up to be peacemakers?"

The Re-creation of Relationship, Interpersonal and Global

The term "re-creation of relationship" reminds us that we are not talking about anything new or unique to the twentieth century. Knowing one another in the love of God at the interpersonal level and at the global level has gone on for thousands of years. Wherever we have records of human experience, this gift for relationship emerges. In one sense we have always known ourselves as a world family.

In some ways it is harder to think of world community and world family today than it was fifty years or one hundred years ago because we are much more aware now of the complexity of the international system. That system has many components which interconnect in many ways. Because it is intellectually paralyzing to try to think about what this means, it is helpful to begin by grounding ourselves in familiar metaphors. The metaphor is a wonderful tool we have for understanding intuitively very complex things. Having created the big picture, we can stand back and learn from the metaphor itself. It can teach us. We can pray about it, we can meditate about it, and we can study it.

The world as a family is a very familiar metaphor indeed. What the metaphor means can fill many books. Vast quantities of demographic data about human beings lie behind the term, but the words "world family" carry a great deal of meaning in themselves. Another metaphor very important to us is that of the world as the Peaceable Garden, or

Peaceable Commonwealth. Every great religious and cultural tradition has had a vision of a Peaceable Garden; this
is not something that arises uniquely in Isaiah. In the
Homeric epics you find the vision of the Peaceable Garden
in the Elysian fields, those green and verdant expanses
where people laid aside their swords and shields and dis-
coursed upon poetry and philosophy. The Koran has images of a green and lovely garden in the desert, where
people live in peace. Concepts of humans laying down
weapons and delighting in one another, delighting in
poetry, delighting in the Creator and in the oneness of
everything are not rare. There is always sharing in these
visions. There is no injustice in the Peaceable Garden.

It is enormously comforting that every civilization has
had this kind of a vision. There is something about the
way we think and dream as human beings that keeps
generating it. And it is good to know that we are like that.
As Christians, the Peaceable Garden is something we share
with the other peoples of the Book, the Old Testament.
We share it with Jews and with the community of Islam.
When we add that in the Garden we are God's family, we
have said something profoundly important. The image of
the family is not complete, however, unless we know in
the deepest sense of knowing that God is our mother as
well as our father. We use the metaphor of God's family
wrongly if we only think of it as a patriarchal family. Let
us use the metaphor for all that it can mean and acknowledge God our mother, and God our father. Let us also
realize that such metaphors can become meaningless
clichés. They can be used in crude and obnoxious ways
that deaden the spirit, or they can be the gateway through
which our prayer life can be entered. They can be the
means for gaining a deeper understanding of our call than
intellectual analysis can provide.

Metaphor is the beginning of vision, and a doorway into
the future. We must consider the task of visioning as an
integral part of our peace work, taking the courage to link
poetic and prophetic visioning with images of the social
and political and economic conditions that might obtain if

we lived in a world without weapons. In working for disarmament, the one major stumbling block we face is that no one really believes we could have a weaponless world. Such a world is just not credible. In fact, we more and more use hedging terms like "a less armed world" and "arms control." General and complete disarmament, which one could talk about uninhibitedly in the early 1940s, is a term we are really embarrassed to use now because it seems so unreal. It seems to suggest we are hiding our heads in the sand. There is a somber aspect to this dilemma. If we cannot delineate in our mind a world without weapons—what relationships would be like, how economic activities would be carried on, how family life would go on, how community life would go on—then we are not serious about disarmament. There is no possibility of moving toward a goal that we cannot even see with our mind's eye.

A basic aspect of working for social change of any kind is the visualization of that which we are working for. We do it all the time for specific community projects; we dream up buildings and we dream up new organizations and we dream up new services. We develop very specific images of them. But few of us have seriously tried the task of delineating in our minds the contours of a weaponless world.

Since the early 1980s, some of us have brought together military personnel, diplomats, United Nations staff, scholars, church people, and community leaders for experiments in visualizing a world without weapons. The concept is to place before people an imaginary *de facto* situation: the weapons are gone. "Now describe the world," we say to the participants. No one is allowed to say it can't happen. We simply state that for the purposes of this exercise, it *has* happened, and the participants must describe the weaponless world they see. It is not easy to help people free up their imaginations, but it can be done.

Once having seen the contours of this future world, we work ourselves back year by year to the present. This way a sense of process and strategy emerges that is quite different from anything you might dream up if you start in the present and ask what we should do now to bring about disarmament. It involves linkage of the tasks of visioning and imagining with the skills of articulating what we know about how society works. This linkage enables us to break through some of the deadlocks and impasses and the sense of helplessness we now experience.

Another task we should try in addition to visioning the social, economic, and political dimensions of the future is the visioning of the religious dimension of a world without arms. What will be the spiritual state of this weaponless world? What will be its religious habits and ways of thinking and being? There are some interesting possibilities in trying to bring our Christian vision into world perspective by putting it alongside the visions for a weaponless world that come out of the communities of Judaism, Islam, Buddhism, and Hinduism. Each of these communities has well-tested methods for conflict resolution, for sharing, and for social justice. We have already taken the Jewish vision of the holy mountain where none shall hurt or destroy, "for the earth shall be full of the knowledge of the Lord" *(Isaiah 11:9)*, as a central vision within Christendom. The kibbutz movement in present day Israel must be appreciated as a serious attempt to re-create the old vision, however one evaluates the political context of that attempt. The Taoists have taught nonviolence for centuries, and the contemporary Buddhist *shramadana* movement, which links spiritual awakening to community action, gives us new insights into peacemaking. The Hindu tradition of *sarvodaya*, seeking the welfare of all through *satyagraha* (nonviolent doing and becoming), and the Islamic concept of the *tauhid*, the loving community of believers that holds the earth's resources in trust for the Creator, can all add to our understanding of the Christian call to peacemaking. The fact that many of the countries where these religious traditions are found are experiencing a great deal of violence tells us that the human race still has a great deal of maturing to do before spiritually-based nonviolence can be effectively practiced.

Obedience, responsibility, and compassion are religious universals. We can draw on these principles with our brothers and sisters of every tradition in building a more peaceful world. And what do we, the Christians, bring? We bring the love of God, made manifest in the life of Jesus. We bring something that is very special to us that we feel makes us different. God has taught the peoples of each religious tradition in the way that they could hear. Each people has its *charismata*, its special manifestations of the Holy Spirit. We are by no means alike. Whatever spiritual unity we can at our best experience comes out of profound diversity. We each bring our particular gifts to the creation of world community, both to imagining a peaceful world and to the making of tools to practice peace.

We already have an important tool for practicing peace across nation-state boundaries: the networks of international nongovernmental organizations (NGOs). More than eighteen thousand groups are organized around religious, cultural, economic, political, and educational purposes, and operate across national boundaries. Each one of these organizations represents a special set of human intentions that reaches across borders to realize a global identity; that is why they are often termed "transnationals." Their purposes transcend the nation-state, and peace is always one of their purposes. Along with peace, they seek understanding, the improvement of the human condition and the furtherance of certain specific human skills. For transnational organizations relating to the arts, the skill would be the fostering of human creativity in the arts. For the Women's International League for Peace and Freedom or the Fellowship of Reconciliation or War Resisters International, it is the skill of creating the conditions for peace.

Everyone is connected with transnational communities, usually in several different ways. For peacemakers, churches and peace organizations are important transnational links. There are hundreds of religious nongovernmental organizations and they are very important to the international peace movement. Each spans some part of the globe. Some of them reach local church communities in as many as 150 countries. Some may not reach more than four or five. Most of them reach thirty, forty, or fifty countries. The World Council of Churches is a federation of Christian NGOs. Other federations include the World Jewish Congress, the World Buddhist Association, the Islamic Assembly, and the interfaith World Conference of Religion and Peace.

Religious NGOs are unique because they are the only ones that potentially reach into every home on the planet. Most organizations have a very selective membership. The women who belong to the Women's International League for Peace and Freedom, for example, are only a tiny fraction of the women in a given country. But if you are talking about the World Council of Churches and its constituent denominational members, you are talking about families in local congregations in the towns and villages of every country of the world.

There is no place too small to have a temple or a church. We know that in this country; it is true abroad as well. To that temple or church come the men, women, and children of the community. As we become aware of the capacity to communicate within and between these transnational religious organizations, we are potentially reaching into individual homes. We are reaching out to men, women, and children where they live. That is not true of any other type of NGO. We have a very unique set of pathways across the planet in our religious transnational organizations. Most people don't think of communication that way. They think of getting important issues before their own parliament. They think of sending resolutions to the United Nations, to heads of other governments, but not to their sister communities around the world.

When we really look at NGOs as our world communication network, we can see how rapidly the net is growing. In 1900 there were several hundred NGOs, and in 1987 there were eighteen thousand. With more organizations come new kinds of sharing, new kinds of information. NGOs are growing in their capacity to carry human caring. They are beginning to carry grassroots concerns.

What do NGOs actually make possible? What goes on in the networks? During the International Year of the Child, some of these NGOs actually trained children between the ages of nine and twelve to go into their own neighborhoods and monitor the illnesses of their own and other households. The children were trained to test water supplies and perform small services which would improve the health of the community. Nine- to twelve-year-olds carry a lot of responsibility in most parts of the world, but their work is not acknowledged. Now NGOs are finally acknowledging the importance of the work of children, and are using their networks to spread skill and training from one country to another. The networks are not only for service, but for learning, for celebration, for human playfulness. They give countless new dimensions to the human identity.

We need to know ourselves in these expanding network identities, for that is how we reach each other from home to home, village to village, town to town. This kind of family-based outreach is the core of our task as peacemakers. Our task isn't just to speak to governments. Our task is to speak to families, to the wise elders, to the children, to the middle-year folks, and use every means at hand to share our visions with others.

The task of peacemaking, however, goes beyond sharing a vision of peace to living a life of peace. That requires practical action skills. If we are to live in "that life and power that takes away the occasion of all wars," as Friends put it, we must figure out how to live our own lives in such a way that the seeds of war are not found there. We take responsibility for an active withdrawal of support from military institutions. This can happen in different ways for different individuals. Generally it takes the form of nonsupport of draft and registration for the draft, and can extend to nonpayment of some or all taxes. In some way, each person who responds to the call takes responsibility for countermanding the military enterprise.

Taking responsibility for removing the seeds of war means going further than nonsupport of the military, how-

ever. We are taken right to the Judaic call to the Jubilee
Year in the Old Testament:

> And ye shall hallow the fiftieth year, and proclaim liberty through-
> out all the land unto all the inhabitants thereof: it shall be a jubilee
> year unto you; and ye shall return every man unto his possession
> and ye shall return every man unto his family. . . . And if thou
> sell ought unto thy neighbor, or buyest ought of thy neighbor's
> hand, ye shall not oppress one another *(Leviticus 25:10,14)*.

This marvelous call to redistribution and social justice was
never carried out in practice in Israel as far as we know,
but the instructions are there. Suddenly the concept becomes fresh for us in these decades as we struggle under
renewed pressure from the Third World to figure out what
a new international economic order would really look like.
It certainly means dealing with the inequities that have
developed through two centuries of industrial revolution.

Nurturing the processes of peace takes more than an
intention to redistribute, however. It takes the skills of
arbitration, mediation, and conflict resolution in the context of the practice of community, of neighboring. We
must develop these skills. Another very important skill
which we in the Christian community haven't given
enough attention to is what I call "prophetic listening."
We all know about prophetic speaking, but prophetic listening means listening to others in such a way that we
draw out of them the seeds of their own highest understanding, their own obedience, their own vision—seeds
that they themselves may not have known were there.
Listening can draw out of people things that speaking to
them cannot. If everybody listened and no one spoke, it
would be a strange world. But prophetic listening is something we might all want to practice.

If we're going to explore prophetic listening we should
look to those who already practice it. We can all think of
such people—they make us feel that we are growing, becoming, just by being in their presence. We grow not
through what they say to us, but by the way they listen
to us. If we are going to practice prophetic listening, there

is a word we will have to eliminate from our vocabulary, especially from our religious vocabulary. That word is "enemy." It appears quite a lot in writings on the issues of war and human imperfection and sin. Sometimes we are trying to deal with God's enemies, those people who are unfaithful or sinful. Sometimes *we* are God's enemy. We have an enormous amount of trouble from this word. An enemy has to be either killed or converted. There really aren't any other things to do with enemies. The word enemy goes with concepts like crusade, or even the Lamb's War. We Quakers know what we mean when we speak of the Lamb's War, but the words sound different on the other side of the world. In fact, the concept of *jihad* in Islam, translated into English as "holy war," can have a meaning very similar to the Lamb's War: a spiritual struggle for the triumph of righteousness over unrighteousness. We interpret this to mean that Islam is warlike, as Islam interprets our concept to mean that Christianity is warlike. Each understands their own spiritual metaphors, but not the spiritual metaphors of the other.

I would like to suggest a new word to replace enemy. The word is "stranger." It's a very old word, and a good one. We have no more enemies but we have strangers. Sometimes we are estranged from ourselves and from God. When we meet a person we call a stranger, that person has to be listened to. We have to find out who he is and what basis for discourse exists. There is no tribal group to my knowledge that does not have a tradition for dealing with the stranger. That is, when a person you have no way of labeling or categorizing appears on the horizon, that person is defined as a stranger. An emissary is sent out to question the stranger until some basis for relationship has been found. When, through lengthy discussion, that basis has been found, the stranger is brought to the community and introduced: "Here is so-and-so, and this is how we are connected to her." Now the former stranger has an identity. This process of dialoguing with a person to find a basis for relationship, not agreement or consensus but simply a basis for relationship, is a widely practiced ritual in many parts of the world. Oddly enough, we have lost it in industrial society. Therefore we have enemies. We don't have rituals for deciding the basis of relationships. The stranger has to be killed or converted.

I suggest that we try to think of those we used to call enemies as strangers and see what it does for our capacity to establish relationship. Jesus taught us how to do this. In all of his dialogues, he never talked with an enemy— never. But he certainly dialogued with strange people. We can learn how to dialogue from the Gospels. If we abolish enemies and dialogue with strangers, then we may be in a position to speak a new word to old quarrels. One of the most troubling things that lies ahead for the world community has to do with quarrels within Islam, much exacerbated by superpower arming of folk societies that until very recently fought face to face with swords. With western technology, they are now destroying each other's resources and peoples at a rate that they do not themselves comprehend. Technology apart, what are these quarrels? We cannot imagine them, much less understand them—in spite of explanatory journalism about Shiites and Sunnis— because we have not dialogued with the community of Islam. One of the most important calls for peacemaking now is for Christian groups to begin dialoguing with the thoughtful and caring leaders of Islamic thought. We need to know, we need to see what the hopes and fears are as they emerge within these internally conflicted societies. Much of their suffering we have helped inflict, through colonialism. It will not be an easy dialogue. During the American hostage crisis in Teheran in 1979, the only Americans trusted by the hostage-holding Iranian students to run a courier service between the hostages and their families back in the United States were members of native American tribes, not white Anglo-Saxon Protestants. Native Americans had never participated in official Western diplomacy. They lived within the borders of, but separate from, the superpower United States. Native Americans had the skill of dialogue, and a shared experience of oppression. The strangers became friends.

We need to learn these skills of dialogue. We cannot go on invading the Holy Lands, as we began doing in the Middle Ages in what we called the Crusades. Neither can we make scapegoats of, or denigrate, the communities of faith that live there. We have ancient, unfinished business with these communities going back a thousand years and more. We share a world, and we must listen to one another.

Another peacemaking task to consider is support of the U.S. Institute of Peace. Efforts must continue to hold the institute faithful to the mandate that established it: create a capacity for nonviolent solutions to international conflict on the part of the United States. In 1979, I served as a member of the committee appointed to hold hearings on whether a U.S. Institute of Peace should be established. I sat with fellow committee members in different halls around the country listening to local people in local communities talk about violence and suffering and oppression as they have experienced them where they live. We heard from homemakers, welfare mothers, teachers, scholars, labor leaders, ministers, community leaders, convicts, Cuban refugees, mediators, veterans, and military officers. We heard from men and women, young and old, from Chicanos, Blacks, native Americans. Each part of the country has its own kinds of local conflict and its own agendas, but everywhere people were able to make the connection between the inability to handle creative peacemaking in their community and the United States' role in the world community. They understood that the United States could not do more as a nation than it could do in Atlanta or Gainesville or Los Angeles or New York. This is rather amazing; we tend to think that people are only concerned with their local affairs. Frankly, I think we expected people to say, "Never mind the international thing—set up something here." But that isn't what they said. They said, "We need a national peace institute and we need one that will also have a regional arm. We want a branch of it in our community."

The committee also visited the military academies. We

went to Annapolis, to West Point, and to the Air Force Academy. At each of those institutions we sat down with the deans and instructors of the social sciences, and the superintendent of the school. We had thoughtful, searching discussions about the appropriate role of the military in national defense. I can tell you that we heard often, in each school, that the military was being seriously misused by Congress, by the United States, by the decision makers on Capitol Hill. These teachers of cadets felt strongly that the combat training they gave was to be a resource of last resort, after all other means of conflict management had failed. They were aware of a whole set of mediation and peacemaking skills that should be brought into play to avoid the necessity of combat. They perceived that these processes were not being pursued, and that the last resort had become too much like a first resort. Each superintendent said, in very much these same words: "When we in the armed services are called into action, our country has failed." That is a powerful statement.

It was very affirming to discover this awareness of the need for peacemaking skills in the military academies. When military officers move from a teaching role in an academy to a strategy role in the Pentagon, they begin looking at situations differently, and forget what they knew when they were teaching cadets. That is the tragedy. At some other point in their lives and in some other corner of their heads they have had real insight into the nature and effectiveness of the military task. One of the hardest challenges any of us has is to carry our best understanding and our highest insights into each situation we enter, not letting some of our wisdom be squeezed out because we are in a setting where power responses seem more appropriate and are being reinforced by those around us.

Now that the U.S. Institute of Peace actually exists, we must remind its board of directors what it was established to do, by providing a steady stream of proposals for training programs in peacemaking and conflict resolution. At present it gives grants to existing universities and centers that do not have their own programs. In time, we can hope it will also provide mid-career retraining to diplomats and to all kinds of people who now work in difficult conflict settings for which they need more skill. We hope it will take all those fine young people who are ready to enter into conflict-resolution careers and give them their initial major training. We hope there will be a research institute that will enable us to test out and make better use of our skills and understandings of conflict and mediation processes, and to grasp the nature of the link between local and global. There is much to be done in order to make the U.S. Institute of Peace that kind of institution.

We are the ultimate interface between the personal and the global. Each of us is the interface. If we understand and pay attention to the connections at whatever point we touch one another, we will be world builders. We don't have to do it all the time, but it is good sometimes to place our daily actions within the context of the planetary networks to which we actually belong through our own individual membership commitments. We can in imagination trace out all the local branches of an organization, and start visualizing the households in a community at whose doors we could knock because they too are members. Because the imagination is a wonderful thing, we can actually knock at those doors. There is a welcome and a pot of tea for each of us in so many thousands of places, when we travel the NGO pathways the human family now has under construction. And we in turn must have our own pot of tea ready for those who knock on our door. If our bodies cannot travel, our voices and our letters can. Each of us is a link between the international and the personal.

The future we envision requires that we travel those pathways with our minds and hearts. Besides visioning, we have much to do. We must work to develop far better peacemaking skills than we now have, including the skills of sharing, of prophetic listening, and of building the institutions we need, such as an effective U.S. Institute of Peace. We must learn the dialogue that turns stranger into friend and makes the word enemy obsolete. All this is hard, for the times are dangerous and frightening, and we are not very wise or clever. But we do nothing alone. Wherever we put our hand or foot, wherever we cast our eyes or tune our ears, God is there and moves with us so that we cannot get lost.

The Family as a Small Society

Our major challenge in the last decade of the twentieth century is to overcome widespread feelings of helplessness and despair over our apparent inability to have any effect on the social processes that grind on around us. We approach the second millennium of the Christian Era overwhelmed with problems of scale and complexity, unsure of the survival of the species itself.

My answer to that challenge is to call attention to the oldest of human groupings, the family. Here is an entity that has met catastrophe after catastrophe over many thousands of years, including the social catastrophes of the rise and fall of civilizations, with a unique combination of inventiveness, courage, and caring. The family group has changed form, structure, and habitat many times, but archaeologists have identified household sites in the Rift Valley of Africa that are more than two million years old.

By focusing on the familial household and calling it a small society, I am separating out the issues of complexity and of scale. E.F. Schumacher said that small is beautiful, but it would not be correct to say that small is simple. Our own bodies are in some ways as complex as the universe itself. We are not ever likely to fully understand the functioning of the thousands of microsystems that maintain our body as a living organism, yet most of the time we can keep it in good working condition and get it to do the things we want it to do. Only in the most exceptional cases of malfunction do we throw up our hands and say, "I am

helpless. I can't make my body work." We have found a
way to live intimately and effectively with our highly complex body system.

Complexity of an unimaginable order also characterizes
the households we live in. Familial households present a
variety of patterns: husband, wife, and children; single
parent and children; lesbian or gay couples with or without
children; a small group of unrelated persons who live com-
munally; or the one-person household with its special ex-
tramural support system. In my terminology, these entities
are all families. I use the term "familial household" to
emphasize the fact that people who live together in households, whatever the arrangement, are in a familial relationship with one another.

The relationships and interactions of these social microsystems are so complex that I as a family sociologist could
never fully capture and record that complexity. One reason
the complexity is unrecordable is that each member of a
household is growing and changing every minute. Each
day, each member has her own unique growth tasks, her
own unique experiences in the world outside—she returns
to the household a different person in the evening than
she was in the morning. Because family members live at
close quarters and must share limited resources, including
space and time, there has to be a continual negotiation
process between them, a continual checking out of
changed circumstances and preferences. We all have very
complex maps in our heads of our familial households. If
we fail to update them daily, we run into problems. Much
family conflict stems from out-of-date mental maps. If we
are a member of a recombined household, we hold an even
more complex map in our heads, including former spouses
and children no longer living with us.

While the complexity of the family is of a high order,
the *scale* is manageable. It is one with which we are comfortable. We call it the "human scale." In the family setting
we get immediate feedback about whether our actions are
producing the result we intend. We get smiles, frowns, or
shrugs; we get a hundred clues as to how we are doing.

The possibility of immediate feedback from behavior characterizes all primary, or face-to-face, groups. It is what makes them so important to our existence as social beings. However, the familial household is a very special form of the primary group, because in the long run it is the one in which we spend the most time. We can manage the complexities of social interaction on the human scale because we get a constant stream of messages about the consequences of our acts. We can dare to experiment, try out new skills, new roles, knowing that we will soon find out if our experiment has worked. Our family will tell us if we are making fools of ourselves!

I propose therefore that we use our experience of the family as a metaphor for society itself, thus giving us a handle on the problem of scale. If we want to make the metaphor more sophisticated, we can say that the family is a reflecting mirror for society, showing in microcosm the customs, mores, structures, institutions, and values of that larger society. Metaphors, however, are dangerous if carelessly used. The family is not simply a mirror, because it has its own independent life. It is not a complete microcosm, a miniature of society, because new structures and roles with emergent properties appear at other system levels as greater numbers of actors are involved.

There is, however, a sound underlying assumption behind the metaphor of the family—one which comes from general systems theory. The assumption is that there are general principles at work in all systems of social interaction, regardless of scale. There are, for example, conflict processes that drive people apart, and there are integrative processes that draw people together. This is true in the family and it is true in the international system. A general systems approach helps us choose what information to ignore in trying to understand complex phenomena. As Kenneth Boulding likes to say, all learning comes through the orderly loss of information. By using the metaphor of the family, we get clues as to what information to throw away in order to understand the functioning of large-scale social systems. At the same time, relevance to the human scale—usefulness for human beings—is introduced as a criterion for judging the functioning of a large-scale system. If a given technology facilitates a social arrangement that helps humans to live joyfully and to handle sorrow and pain without being psychically destroyed, then it is, in E.F. Schumacher's terms, an appropriate technology. Schumacher's great gift to us in his "small is beautiful" concept is the recovery of the human scale, of human feelings of self-efficacy, well-being, and joyfulness as primary social values. This makes possible the development of new ways to test social and physical technologies.

We will begin exploring the family metaphor by seeing how the household functions as a small society: shaping people, culture, social values, and physical products.

The household as a society has population, resources, culture, technology, boundaries, and environment. Its form of political organization may be patriarchal, matriarchal, or egalitarian. Its decisions on allocation of scarce resources are only as participatory as its political organization allows. It may have a subsistence economy, or be linked to a high-tech industrial or postindustrial information economy involving daily export of people and daily import of information, money, and goods. There may be a highly differentiated division of labor between ages and sexes, or a low differentiation with task sharing inside the home and job sharing outside the home. Food, money, clothes, and possessions are generally shared between members, though not necessarily equally. Most members provide some form of health care to other members as needed, over time, with women and children being the chief caregivers. Listening and counseling services are available with varying frequency. Play and recreation activities are conducted partly in the home, partly outside. Civic activities by members are directed to the maintenance of a community environment comfortable for the household.

Every one of these activities requires skill in negotiation and sharing. Since the members of this society live in close quarters, the constant requirements for negotiation would be infuriating if there were not something called affection to hold this society together. In the negotiation process, authority and power give some members more weight than others. The American ideal of familial power relations is slowly moving from a patriarchal to an egalitarian model, but the ideal is more often honored in the breach than the observance. Lesbian and gay households have a particular role to play in helping our society develop familial egalitarianism, since there is no obvious authority figure in such households. Lesbian and gay relationships tend to be more finely tuned with regard to decision making and responsibility sharing than most male-female relationships.

That fine tuning is hard work in any family, even when there is a lot of affection present. The truth is that the familial society is not very successful at carrying out its tasks. Every one of us carries a load of resentment from childhood, resentment both at parents and at siblings, for burdens they have put upon us in the past. In live-together households, resentments accumulate as much as in contractual and kin households. There are times when we intensely dislike our families. When conflicts become acute, households break up. We must be honest about the fact that the family as an exemplar of loving and caring between humans is frequently a fiction. Yet the fiction is an important one because, like all fiction, it tells a story. The story is about longing to be "at home" in our own special place, accepted by our own special people. It is both a longing for relationship, and a longing to arrange our environment and have it stay the way we want it to be. A house and a garden may be a one-room apartment and a flower pot, but we have arranged it. Relationships cannot be so easily arranged, yet the need for relationship is even stronger than the need for place. In our feelings for those close to us, we swing between love tinged with awe and an impatient desire to have the other fit into our program, our needs. Because both feelings are intense, we must learn to walk the narrow ridge Martin Buber speaks of between "I-thou" relationships and "I-it" relationships with those we love. Sometimes it is enough that they—the beloved other—simply *be*. Other times we need them in very specific ways; they become instruments of our survival.

The failures in relationships are failures to walk this narrow ridge. That it is hard to do is not a reason not to try, not an argument against families. As humans we really do not have any choice in this matter. Humans thrive only in primary living groups. They cannot be successfully reared in communal nurseries, or kept perpetually in dormitories. The reappearance of familial groups in the Israeli kibbutzim is one evidence among many of the need for the *intimate* group. The problems of familial relations only serve to underline the basic fact that it is hard to grow up human. The household is a living-learning experiment in which the skills of human relationship *may* be learned. It is also an experiment in which one learns to occupy, arrange, and adapt to one's environment, including nature. The home terrain is the human scale in its basic form. It is the place for dreaming about human purposes and ultimate meanings.

It is great comfort to me, when I get discouraged about the state of humanity, to realize that every civilizational tradition, no matter how warlike or materialistic its history, contains in its literary record imagery concerning a Peaceable Garden. The Peaceable Garden is a public space, often a garden or green meadow, where people have laid aside weapons and live together in peace: feasting, playing, talking philosophy, and reciting poetry. The Greeks knew it, the battle-happy warriors of northern Europe knew it, the desert Bedouin knew it. We have an enduring capacity to visualize humans as better than we experience ourselves to be and the social order as more harmonious than what we see around us. We also find hardy spiritual adventurers in every age, who respond to the vision by trying to reshape their lives and their society.

Sometimes those spiritual adventurers are loners, but more often they are family-identified. The exodus of the Christians in the third, fourth, and fifth centuries—from the cities of the Roman Empire to found new communities in the Egyptian and Syrian deserts—was a record of family enterprises: brother-sister, parent-child, and husband-wife, with brother-sister teams predominating. The sisters of St. Augustine and St. Anthony are two of many such teams who headed religious communes. A Benedictine monastery is as much a family as husband-wife-children are a family, and the Rule of St. Benedict explicitly states the familial character of the individual houses of the order.

There is a lot of talk about social transformation in these times. There are those who expect us simply to "evolve" into higher-order beings, or who think we have already evolved and no one has noticed. The spiritual visionaries who have preceded us, however, always pointed out that a lot of hard work is involved. The Benedictines have been working at it for centuries. The familial household is a place where the work of becoming can begin. Every newly formed household can be seen as a colony of heaven, where the work of forming new persons is undertaken.

The household is also where the work of forming a new society begins. The Anabaptist tradition in Europe, out of which Methodism and the historic peace churches came, has its roots deep in the Middle Ages, in familial subcultures such as the Family of Love and the Brethren of the Common Life. The children of these subcultures learned to accept revilement and prison for their beliefs as badges of honor, then as now. The twentieth-century peace movement of the West represents a pronounced continuity with those older familial subcultures, including Hasidic, Catholic, and Greek Orthodox as well as Anabaptist subcultures of nonviolence. Values and skills appropriate to the non-violent resolution of conflict at every level from familial to international have been transmitted in family subcultures from generation to generation. Even today, some of the best materials for teaching children to handle social conflict nonviolently come from these groupings. The Children's

Creative Response to Conflict Program was started in the 1960s by the New York Yearly Meeting of the Religious Society of Friends and is now administered by the Fellowship of Reconciliation in Nyack, New York. Within the Catholic church there is the National Parenting for Peace and Justice Network. Both programs produce conflict-resolution materials for children and families.

The antiwar movement of the 1960s appeared anti-familistic, but further research suggests far more continuity with family values than at first appeared. The parents of the antiwar generation were more often than not survivors of the quietism of the 1950s who kept their dissenting values intact. Many peace demonstrations in the 1960s were in fact family demonstrations. Women's Strike for Peace was a familial movement, based on a concern for children; grandmothers, mothers, and children demonstrated together. This familial character of peace demonstrations continued right through the violence of the 1970s, and is still evident in the demonstrations of today.

The contemporary environmental movement is at least as familistic as the peace movement. This relates to the fact that the family is the only social system in which resource limitations and consequences of different types of resource utilization provide immediate feedback to the behaving social unit. Recycling and energy conservation represent a series of tangible acts with consequences for a household. The psychological satisfaction of successful conservation strategies for a family has encouraged people to apply what they have learned in household and neighborhood to larger social issues. Though the systems involved are more complex and the consequences more diffuse, environmentalists are nevertheless among the most successful activists we have today, suggesting that household-level insights are relevant for larger-scale problems.

Experience tells us that the family is indeed a workshop in which solutions to social problems can be tried out, and that historically, family subcultures developed social interests that extended far beyond their personal well-being.

Now we will look at the particular activities of the household society that may be important to the development of a healthy localism in the larger society.

Recovery of the Joy of Work

The leisure society with its emphasis on labor saving has misled people into thinking that work is a necessary evil and not to be enjoyed. One avenue to the recovery of the joy of work lies in the household, since much activity there is, of necessity, labor intensive, and is done *with the hands.* It has long been noted that rural families, though they work harder, longer hours than urban families, are more satisfied with their way of life and report themselves happier than their urban brothers and sisters. In a series of observations of farm families in Vermont, Colorado, and Oklahoma, I confirmed the very deep pleasure that farm families take in their farm life. The children begin chores at the age of four, the wife works as a partner to her husband, and the fact that everyone works together is usually cited as one of the things liked best about farm life. Seeing the fruits of their labors growing under their eyes is another primary source of satisfaction.

Urban families seeking that same experience are finding places to grow food in the city; home gardening is on the increase everywhere. Prisons and mental hospitals use garden plots as therapy. Local food production by household units seems both therapeutic and economical; many associated craft skills are picked up in the process.

The reversal of the historic rural-urban migration in the United States over the past two decades, with a net population outflow back to villages and open country, suggests that this discovery of the joy of physical labor is being acted on in very concrete ways. Redividing domestic tasks among all household members as women become an accepted part of the permanent labor force, rather than pin-money part-timers, provides more opportunities for men and children to discover the satisfaction of household craft.

The "I hate housework" sentiment that fueled the women's movement now needs rephrasing as "We like to work as a household team." The more skilled the labor, the more the pleasure; this brings sewing, carpentry, and other crafts to the center of attention again.

Scott Burns predicts that there will be a shift toward home production of everything that can possibly be produced there for both economic and lifestyle reasons. From my own observations in rural areas and small towns, children gravitate toward oldsters who are willing to take time to teach craft and machine-tool skills, just because they like knowing how to do things. Children who only know how to work computers have a very narrow range of skills.

Learning as a Family Enterprise

In Japan in the early 1960s, I discovered that Japanese women were among the best educated in the world because they supervised the studies of their sons (and sometimes daughters) right through college and graduate school, studying ahead so they could test their children. Education was a family enterprise! The tendency on the part of American parents to turn all education over to the schools is now reversing, with increasing numbers of parents either keeping their children at home and doing the teaching themselves, or becoming involved in school learning programs. The dissatisfaction with what schools are doing generalizes to a dissatisfaction with how growing-up time is spent both inside and outside the home.

Parents sometimes have very hard choices to make between family time and working-outside-the-home time, but at least now the values of alternative time use are being carefully considered. Community-sponsored workshops on how to learn as a family, how to play as a family, and how to solve conflicts as a family are supporting new trends to value time spent with the family group, and to become more involved in one another's social, intellectual, and spiritual maturation.

Self-initiated learning—organized by the learner without the aid of a conventionally taught class or workshop—has been greatly underestimated. Alan Tough's research in Canada on self-initiated learning indicates that the average family member of any age from youth to older years spends two hundred hours each year on some self-organized learning project at home, such as learning to sew, learning a new language, or learning to play the guitar. All in all, probably more learning goes on at home than in any other place where we spend time.

Health and Welfare Self-Help

Home doctoring by parents and siblings, and nursing care for the sick, have always been ninety-nine percent family activities, with doctors on hand chiefly for emergencies. The shift in the 1950s and 1960s to doctor dependency for the middle class has now moved back toward more self-help. This time, the availability of workshops, publications, and health centers offering education in nutrition and health care helps families become more knowledgeable about staying healthy.

Communication skills workshops for parents and teenagers and husbands and wives, enabling them to handle their own problems, are replacing dependency on long-term professional counseling. The marriage encounter movement is one of the most remarkable of the self-help movements. It spread from coast to coast in the United States over a fifteen-year period with no professional or administrative staff whatsoever, simply on the basis of the principle that couples who have experienced an encounter weekend help organize a similar weekend for others in their community. This movement has learned to tap the love that married partners feel for each other, but have forgotten how to express. By disentangling themselves from human-services bureaucracies, families are taking back their own households and re-creating their own lives on a human scale.

One mutual aid system has always operated outside of human-services bureaucracies and continues to do so: the extended family. Relatives in separate households—living nearby or far away—have always been part of the family health-care system in times of serious illness. Financial emergencies have also been handled within the extended family to a significant degree through intrafamilial grants of money. This critical life-support system is almost completely invisible to the public eye.

Children, even quite young children, have been more important in helping to meet family crises than is recognized by professionals or parents. In an exploratory study done in the late 1970s, I could not find a single college-age student who did not remember having helped a parent through a serious crisis such as illness, bereavement, unemployment, alcoholism, or spouse abuse—sometimes at the age of four or five.

The rural-urban migrations that accompanied the industrialization process in the United States were more than migrations from country to city. They were migrations from relatively self-sufficient households, where all family members shared in productive labor and the teaching of necessary skills to younger members, to urban areas lacking in the materials for self-help. Family crises in the countryside were generally met by self-help. In the city there was more dependency on the helping professions. This varied by class, however. The urban working poor were more apt to continue extended family self-help in the city than the middle class. Middle-class decline in self-help and subsequent dependency on the helping professions were striking by mid-century. The reversal of the rural-urban trend and the rise of self-help activities in the middle class suggest a possible change in middle-class consciousness, however slight the indications may be at present.

The rise in self-help activities does seem to reflect a rejection of earlier feelings of helplessness. Buffeted by the larger social system over which they have no control, families are beginning to take hold of their lives at the system level at which they can have control—their own households. This could be seen as a retreat from complexity, or as a potential launching pad for further social-change activity. We will explore a particular example of household activity contributing to social change at the local level.

My perspective on the household as an active source of social change rather than an expiring victim of modernization is in part due to several years of observing household behavior in boomtown settings in the Colorado Rockies. The energy boomtown is one of the least-desirable places to live for families accustomed to the amenities of suburbia. The newcomer family finds that nothing is right. The town is far from urban areas, usually located in a fragile mountain ecosystem. The housing is too small and too expensive, the streets too dirty, the schools too crowded and outdated, the store goods outrageously priced. There is nowhere to go except bars, nothing to do except drink. People aren't friendly. No wonder divorce, suicide, alcoholism, and crime rates go up in boomtowns. If newcomer families can develop active community roles under such conditions they can hardly be accused of a retreat into privacy.

The first task of the newcomer family is to build itself a series of supports for keeping physically afloat in the new community. Adult males have instantaneous help from the workplace. School children have a harder time; they need to find a niche in a potentially hostile school environment, where new kids are seen as adding to overcrowding and competing for places on athletic teams. Wives have the hardest time of all. For survival they keep grounded in the town left behind through extensive use of the phone and the mails, while exploring the new town and grasping at whatever meager social contact is first available.

Family members go through a series of stages in the community bonding process. Every step of the way may be discussed over the family dinner table. Children advise parents, parents advise children. Collective family wisdom is very important. Churches, social groups, hobby clubs, civic organizations, and mutual aid groups of various kinds are tested out and discarded or joined. For some families, the whole process is handled in six months. For others, it may take several years.

At some point, the family becomes inventive in its adaptation process. In the first wave of Colorado boomtowns in the 1880s, families literally faced nothingness; they had to create every amenity from scratch—home, newspaper, school, church, store. The inventions were all family enterprises, and even today the stores on the Main Streets of those old boomtowns (now going through a second or third energy boom) reflect the whole-family character of the enterprises in their early days. Grandparents and young couples and school-age children all wait on customers together.

The newcomer families I observed between 1977 and 1981 became active in two kinds of social inventions, in response to the cultural barrenness of their new environment relative to the urban area they had left behind. Both types of activity involved whole-family participation. One was literal construction of new facilities and new organizations locally: remodeling an old barn to become a cultural center housing local art exhibits and a concert series; building or raising funds for new parks, recreation facilities, and swimming pools; starting a craft center; organizing new athletic teams; starting a community counseling-service clinic or hospital.

The other type of social invention was communication and transportation networks which brought community residents—particularly children—to major cultural opportunities at the nearest urban center (two to three hours' drive away), and special art, music, and dance teachers to the community to give lessons. Medical and other special services were made available through the same kind of transportation networks. These communication and transportation networks were very complex, sometimes involving hundreds of people, and took a lot of entrepreneurial time to organize. Tasks in the network were taken on by family units, with men as fully involved as women.

This kind of networking often led newcomers to the state agricultural extension service, which usually has active programs in boomtown areas. As newcomer families from urban areas became involved in the whole-family style activities of 4-H clubs, where fathers and mothers attend their children's 4-H skill-training sessions, their mental horizons began extending to the rural environs of the boomtown. The newcomers also discovered statewide activity networks through such experience. For long-term environmental planning, this extension of horizons through whole-family activities builds an infrastructure of concerned households that will make their views felt at local and national levels.

Whole-family involvement in community activities makes possible a holistic view of community needs, and lengthens the time horizon of immediate concern. The family asks: What will it be like here for our children, now preschoolers, by the time they are in high school? Will this be a good place to live?

Not every newcomer family was able to engage in the kinds of activities I have described. Some retreated into apathy, some just gave up and left. But it is important to know that some families can become active community shapers under difficult and stressful conditions.

The point has been made that the family is a highly complex, small-scale system which offers its members opportunities to act effectively within the household and the local community. Can the localist skills the family develops be useful in larger scale systems? More importantly, can the values of human scale be protected as individual humans move into larger-scale tasks? Before answering these questions, I would like to offer some reflections on the context in which the family interacts with the larger world. The contradictory trends of giantism and localism, and of contrasting types of localism, make the family/world interface a very complex one.

It is ironic that the feverish corporate mergers into megacorporations and the continued expansion of an already dinosaurian military system constitute a ballet danced to the music of a new localism. The New Right's New Federalism, the electronic cottage-as-workplace movement, the popularity of do-it-yourself kits, and the E.F. Schumacher Society are all melodic lines in the new music. In other words, very diverse sets of voices are calling for an end to hierarchy, bureaucracy, and large-scale organizations as inappropriate to the needs of the new age.

Most of the voices for localism, however, call for a high-technology approach that leaves the individual as dependent on the highly specialized skills of others as before, the difference being thàt the skills are now available via home computer. John Naisbitt predicts that people will increasingly compensate for their dependence on machines by spending more time in consumer-focused public spaces. He calls this "high tech/high touch":

> The more technology we introduce into society, the more people will aggregate, will want to be with other people: movies, rock concerts, shopping. Shopping malls, for example, are now the third most frequented space in our lives, following home and workplace.

The yearning of people for people is real, and should be acknowledged with seriousness and respect. But the kind of localism Naisbitt describes strikes me as the localism of sheep huddling together. Yet Naisbitt also emphasizes the development of self-help skills and local political initiative, using locally available high-tech resources. Implicit but undiscussed in his study are the contradictions between consumerism and localism. Consumerist localism is decentralized distribution of the products of a tightly meshed set of production systems which operates through the more familiar decision-making pyramids. It is a far cry from the localism of "Buddhist economics," which emphasizes production from local resources for local needs, aiming at the maximum of well-being with the minimum of consumption, and based on a conception of work as a means of purification of human character. It is also a far cry from the localism of the family as a small society, which calls for an authenticity and depth of relationship between family members and between family and community which cannot be achieved in shopping malls and rock concerts.

This more grounded localism is another distinct, if faint, voice in the localist chorus. It is the purpose of the E.F. Schumacher Society to help make that voice louder. There are men and women everywhere who long for this kind of localism, and writers, such as Marilyn Ferguson and Duane Elgin, who have articulated their longings. Two serious problems confront us in working for authentic and grounded localism. One is to understand high-tech localists and find ways to work with them without losing sight of deep value differences. The other is to understand and deal with the stranglehold giantism has on our society even as new localist trends are developing.

Giantism is a complex phenomenon, with roots in the concept of the modern nation-state as a democratic institution requiring the replacement of an elite military force with mass people's armies to defend it. It happened that these enlarged military forces were the first social entities to develop the skills of large-scale movement of people and material. Armies had to develop these skills in order to carry out the functions assigned to them by governments. Increasingly, governments came to rely on armies for large-scale operations of any kind. Soldiers were the "scale specialists" who could do mass evacuations and mass feedings. The civilian sector never developed comparable skills, so the expertise stayed in the military. Because that expertise became more and more necessary for planning as governments became more complex, military personnel shifted from the category of resources-on-call to the status of co-planners and policy makers. This shift happened in the mid-1950s in the United States.

This explains, in very oversimplified terms, how foreign policy has come to be approached in terms of military rather than diplomatic action in present national security thinking. Military action must be centrally planned and carried out in secrecy. This means that organizational innovations involving localism and networking can be applied only to a limited extent. Today, each modern industrial state is pinned under the burden of a large centrally planned and hierarchically organized military force in an era when social problems call for local initiative and nonhierarchical information flows. Burdensome and inefficient as the defense systems are, and irrelevant to the difficult political conflicts they are supposed to deal with, it will nevertheless take very substantial and prolonged local initiatives to "transarm" nation-state systems. The transarmament concept, developed by Gene Sharp, is an ingenious device for a complete reconstitution of defense systems without evoking the terror of helplessness that the term "disarmament" evokes.

Unfortunately, automation of military systems has made it possible to handle very great complexities centrally—albeit badly. Security systems on a human scale will come about only when high skill levels have been achieved in the productive management of conflict between individuals and groups, from the local community to the international community. If localism does not develop such skills, it cannot "save" us.

Oddly enough, the megacorporation and the giant military machine are neither of them "global" in the *planetary* sense of being rooted in the community of earth. Such power systems, which serve institutions rather than human beings, are better termed "gigantic." Human households and face-to-face groupings and more complex social networks across the globe are planetary. A term for the sum total of these groupings might be *sociosphere*—the web of human connections that enfolds the globe. We must reclaim the word "global" from the institutions of corporate and military power, give it back its planetary meaning, and return it to the networks that operate on a human scale.

Planetary networks linking households already span the globe through the mechanism of transnational nongovernmental organizations (NGOs) formed over the past hundred years in many areas of human interest and concern—economic, political, cultural, and religious. Every single transnational organization, whether it has to do with poetry, organic gardening, parenting, conflict resolution skills, religious faith, or the conditions of human labor, ultimately links *households*. People in their wholeness as men and women, as members of caring households, reach out to the wholeness of others they will never see, and affirm a common goal, a common fate.

In the global systems class I taught at Dartmouth College, I had each student identify all the transnational NGO memberships represented in their family, through their own activities and the activities of their parents, siblings, uncles, aunts, perhaps grandparents. These usually include Scouts, church organizations, professional associations, and hobby organizations, among others. Students then studied the purposes of each NGO and its distribution of national sections across the planet, and mapped that distribution. I told them to keep their maps, because in every country containing an NGO in which one of their family is involved, there are a number of households where they will be welcome, as a part of the same community of concern. This is planetary localism.

The NGOs, like familial households, hardly begin to realize their potential for human growth and development. They need a lot of effort poured into them. They particularly need more cultivation of the vision that brought them into being, so their members can remember the high purposes that could guide their lives. In workshops designed to help people imagine a future world without weapons, the NGO theme emerges again and again, although people do not use that terminology. Once people start imagining how a world would function without military security systems, they immediately start thinking about how to connect local households and local communities around the globe. The nation-state seems of little relevance when the focus is on fostering human peaceableness and joy.

Rather than bewail the human weaknesses and the socioeconomic and political constraints that assail the potentials for human betterment contained in familial households, I would rather celebrate the potential itself. In the household we have a place to stand, a place to work at being human, to work at humanizing the planet, a place where love can break in. It is a place where we can begin functioning right now, just as we are, with what we know at this moment. We need no grants or subsidies, no changed laws, to begin the work of humanization. Perhaps we will discover that we are not alone, that the planet is God's household, and that the work of becoming human is the work of opening to God's presence every moment we walk the earth.

The Family as a Way
into the Future

The future of the family is a subject often approached with great anxiety in these times. I propose to strike a new tone of inquiry, and to ask what discoveries lie before us about the family. Since family-type togetherness is the oldest human experience, it is not unlikely that what lies ahead for us will be arrived at in the context of having been formed as persons in family-type settings. As a futurist, I have long been convinced that families are the primary agents of social change in any society. It is in this setting that individuals first become aware that the passage of time means growth and change, that tomorrow is never like yesterday. It is in this setting that one's first daydreams about a different future take place. I have come to find "the Tao of family" a meaningful way to describe the special nature of family as directioned movement. Tao means "the way," and the Tao of family is the Way of family into the future. In this view, the family is not a barrier between us and a better society, but a path to it.

The present ambivalence about whether the family is a good institution for human beings stands in sharp contrast to earlier idealization of the family. There is a social myth that in some past golden age families were totally devoted to one another, totally sufficient to each other's needs (with the extended family hovering benignly in the background to shore up any possible weaknesses in time of trouble). One extreme reaction to this myth is to say that in our era, family life is all pain and no devotion, producing an essential, tragic loneliness in each of its members. The truth lies somewhere between the two extreme positions. It is useful to call attention to the fact that family life is a difficult, demanding way of life. However, the "new realism" offers no key to understanding the mysterious desires, impulses, and interdependencies that have brought humans together in family-type groupings as far back as we can go in archaeological and paleontological searches. Do present divorce rates, escalating family violence, and rising levels of youth drug abuse, alcoholism, suicide, and flight from home signal some great historic change in how humans will deal with their most intimate as well as most public wants and needs? Is there really some better arrangement than the family almost within sight that will produce better human beings, more economic justice, and peace instead of war?

It is tempting to think that we could design structural arrangements for the nurture of human beings that would be proof against eruptions of folly and violence in thought and deed, arrangements that would guarantee the production of individual and social goodness. And indeed, many structural modifications can be made in social arrangements to make life more peaceful and just for communities and nations. The art of social design is at least ten thousand years old—as old as the oldest town. But social design always misses the uniqueness of the individual human being. Art and religion alike spring from the basic clash between social prescription as embodied in law, custom, and culture and the living, throbbing human being whose case does not fit the prescription. Social prescriptions never fit. If we have the illusion that they do, it is because all of us, with a practiced skill that makes the effort invisible to other eyes, are continually modifying our milieu to suit our own ways of being and doing. We push at the edges of custom daily by performing our various roles in our own special way, with our elaborations, our omissions, and our own inner reservations. If each of us had to push continuously at the edges of custom alone and unaided, it would be an exhausting task. People who are really alone in a society, both socially and spiritually, give up on that basic task of individuation-in-community. They are the anomic, the alienated ones.

The family is an ancient social invention which provides support for the individuation process. Whether one is surrounded by the bureaucratic webs of ancient empires or modern governments, or simply by tribal councils and village mores, there are spaces inside those public webs taken up by family-type formations, sheltering their members against the harshness of social prescription. There are forms of the Tao—the inner structure of all being—that can never be found in the web itself, but only in these spaces.

In times of rapid social change such as the present, the shelters do not function very well, and many individuals flee them as if they were prisons instead. Entering the web itself, the would-be escapees may come to feel trapped in the mazes of professional human services provided by social workers, therapists, and correctional workers trying to do what the family failed to do. There has always been a third way, however, in all societies undergoing rapid change, and that has been the experimental creation of new family forms or the modification of existing ones. The commune as an alternative family form has been invented over and over again, bringing persons together to live as a household whose members are not otherwise related. Some communes, such as the monastic communities of the Hindu, Buddhist, Christian, and Moslem faiths, have lasted for nearly two thousand years, each generation taking in young children born outside the community to rear as members. Secular communes, often born of war and depression, are usually more short-lived. They frequently involve the merging of several previously separate groupings, as was the case with the *frèrèche*, a kind of extended-family household in medieval Europe. All-women communes, such as those run by the religiously oriented laywomen of the Beguine movement, eased the rural-to-urban movement of single women in the later Middle

Ages. Some took in children, some did not. In European history, there has been a steady stream of experimental communes for men and women in alternative-to-marriage types of arrangements, side by side with the chaster experiments of celibate communes, from the time of the millennial peasant uprisings associated with the end of feudalism to the present. The history of these experiments puts the experiments of our own times into proper perspective.

Most experimental communes, then as now—particularly those not based on deep religious conviction—tended to be short-lived. The reason is not far to seek. A commune is even more demanding than a kinship family in terms of skill in social relations and the need for continuous sensitivity to others. Relations can never be taken for granted. They must be exhaustingly re-created each day, and most people are not prepared for that kind of effort. Much writing about the family today implies that for the first time in history there are a lot of alternative lifestyles available to people which are easier than family living and more exciting than anything ever known before. Nothing could be further from the truth. First, the experiments are demanding, and second, industrialization and modern urbanization have, if anything, narrowed the range of available variations in lifestyles. The experiments generated by the vast uprootings in Europe—brought about by a combination of the Crusades and the end of feudalism, by bad harvests lasting over decades with resulting food shortages, illness, and plague, and by the simultaneous rise of a new urban craft technology offering new work for the rural unemployed—are a rich part of our heritage unrecorded in the standard histories of western civilization.

Even in more settled times, there have been many varieties of household patterning. While a certain proportion of any population lives in households that are standard for that society—whether the matrilineal households of Kerala, India, the two-to-three-wife multihouseholds of rural Nigeria, or the patrilineal single-residence households of Euro-North America—more sophisticated demographic analysis is showing us that fewer people live in these standard households than had been thought. In most societies, up to one-third of women are either unmarried or widowed, many of them with children, and their needs contribute to the creation of alternative patterns. Again, since alternative arrangements are harder to maintain, they are often short-lived. They nevertheless attempt to sustain long-term involvement in nurturing between adults and children.

During times of trouble, ad hoc arrangements multiply. In quieter times, the range of alternative solutions narrows, and a larger proportion of the population once again lives in simpler family-type households. This happens because the alternatives are costly. We are getting signals of discontent with the costs of alternatives right now in our own society. One such signal is found in the number of couples with no mutual legal commitments who are suing each other in courts of law, presumably for not honoring the very commitments the nonlegal relationship was to keep them free from in the first place. Commitment always crops up as a fundamental human yearning. It is hard for true individuality to flourish in a milieu that lacks attentive others who can mirror back the growth of one's individuality over time. Families seem to provide a remarkably effective instrument for such mirroring back, and thus for the production of sustainable individuality in human beings.

We worry far too much about the *form* of the family, as if, in spite of all the variations present in history, there should be one optimum pattern answering the human condition. We underestimate people's capacity to respond to their own social experience. Today, many people who are finding the single-parent household a very difficult form of family life are trying to do something about it. Neighborhood and community-level inventions directed to creating extended-family type support networks for these hard-pressed adults are a logical development, one that Friends meetings should take care to support. The single-parent family, as I have already pointed out, is not new. There have always been widows, widowers, and unmarried women rearing children. What *is* new is that the concepts of neighborhood and community have been weakened, and the physical proximity of extended families made less probable, by greater geographical mobility. Yet the history of this country is a history of one long migration. The re-creation of neighborhood and adoption of a new extended family is only what every migrant family has always had to do.

The two-parent family is also being inventive, moving away from a cramping "woman-in-the-home-only" image that was, in fact, merely a temporary adaptation to industrialization and the termination of preindustrial partnerships of women and men in family workshops or on family farms. The return of women to the work force in the current phase of the industrial era has, however, required a redefinition of family roles. Parenting and household maintenance are now both male and female responsibilities. Different concepts of male and female personhood are thus required. The personhood of the young and of the old has also had to be redefined as we gain a better understanding of human capacity and social needs over the life span. One of the most challenging new social lessons is that ageism is as cramping to human beings as sexism or racism. The family upheavals we see today are part and parcel of this tremendously accelerated learning process, and should not be simplistically labeled symptoms of social decay.

Still, the nagging doubt remains for many people: is the family a thing of the past, or is it still a significant human enterprise? And will it continue to be so in the future? I have already suggested that household forms have been resilient in the past in response to changing conditions. Now I would like to show what households will continue to be uniquely equipped to do for the human condition, if we grasp the vision of the family as a special form of continuous creation in society. It should be understood that by "family," I refer to any household grouping which involves adults and children in continuing commitment to each other over time. There may be one, two, or more adults, in couples or singly or a combination of the two.

They may be heterosexual, gay, or celibate, with from zero to many children. (The possibility of children is important to the concept of family, but a certain percentage of households remain childless in every society.)

What makes the household a family is that each member will care about each other member and be available in time of need, with no expiration date on that availability. This includes a commitment to sharing the experience of facing death, something we do not talk enough about as a family commitment. In the case of divorced and remarried combinations, the concept of continued availability to past spouses and children to meet the crises of life and death still holds in principle. While the bitterness surrounding divorce sometimes makes this impossible, most divorced persons do in fact continue to be helpful to one another in some way. Single-person households can also be included under the rubric of "family," particularly if the individual makes home a center for a network of nonresident friends and relatives, and defines these relationships in terms of long-term commitment. Not infrequently, single persons contribute more to family-type bonding than a family indifferent to its own being, because they care, and spend time showing that they care.

Family life is an act of continuous creation—the creation of human beings and of the society in which they live. Creation is at once solemn and reckless. It is both a reflection of the divine order and a uniquely individual act. The word "Tao" embodies theses contradictions better than any word we have in our own language. Tao is the divine order, yet it is also a way. It is stillness and non-action, a standing in the light, yet it is also all movement, all action. It is God the Creator, and God the Uncreated. Family life, on the other hand, may seem by its very nature to be action, movement, shaping. This equating of the family with action causes us much trouble. We think we must be *doing* the right things. There are few voices that speak to family *being*. The seemingly effortless quality of the fulfilled family (only seeming, mind you!) is based on a rootedness in being which infuses all doing. Quaker family culture is

richly blessed with opportunities for rootedness in the
practices of silent waiting and shared stillness—in the development of an at-homeness with others that does not
depend on verbal communication. These are family practices, not just meeting practices, and no meeting silence
can be any deeper than the family silences it draws upon.
Beyond the shared quiet is, of course, the individual quiet,
and in a spiritually alive community there is still seepage
of the spirit from individual to family to meeting and back
again.

Now I will speak of my understanding of family life as
creation and being.

The family is a dance of growth. Each member is one
day older each day, moving a different body, seeing with
different eyes, thinking and feeling with a new mind and
heart, from infant to grandparent. For the dance to go on,
each member must be daily attuned to the changing body
signals of each other member. There is a lot of humor in
the dance. Clothes never quite fit, feet grow too big, voices
squeak, middle-aged bodies sway uncertainly, stiffness
makes marionette-walking part of the dance for the elderly.
Part of the humor lies in the fact that each of us is dancing
as if everyone else were yesterday's person, yet knowing
all the while that we are today's. Daily, belatedly, each of
us makes lightning-quick adjustments because, after all,
no one is yesterday's person. A world has happened since
yesterday, and has left its traces on each mind and body.
How does anyone ever recognize anyone else in a family?
In the outside world we can get by with projecting and
responding to stereotypes—ritualized versions of the self
that vary by decades rather than by days. Not so in the
family. It is the only setting in which we must remain close
to others far apart from us in temperament and age.

And yet for all the irritation, scorn, and derision over
the acting-up (always seen as exaggerated in the others—
but never, of course, in ourselves), the magic of the dance

still creates its own understandings. We make room for the big feet, the theatrical gesture, the new sad limp. Family interaction is a dialectic of drooping shoulders and whooping new identities. New furniture changes the physical staging of family life; so does the continuous process of acquiring new clothes in new sizes. The table is set with different foods as nutritional requirements change in the growth process. Different spaces for sleep and rest must be left for each family member as bodily needs for dreaming and dreamlessness change. "Rights" to physical and social space subtly alter and are traded around the family over time. Sometimes the dance is punctuated by explosions; the staging doesn't change fast enough, or someone refuses to go along with this particular day's reality. Mother has gone back to school, or has a new job. Sister has her first newspaper route. Father has been laid off at work. There are so many forcible intrusions on the family ballet. Rude as the jolts may be, if new rhythms can be improvised in time, much bitterness dissolves in the sheer movement of the dance. Sometimes the dance breaks down entirely. But for the most part, this incredible person-creating dance of family life goes on. Each creates the other in the family ballet. No one may sit it out, as we can elsewhere.

I am using the dance as a metaphor, and yet it is more than a metaphor. More families than we suspect do impromptu dancing for sheer joy. Folk dancing makes a wonderful form of family ballet. In my own childhood, Swedish gymnastics, led exuberantly by my mother on early summer mornings by the sea, was a much-loved form of family ballet. All movement is dance, if we but see it that way. We may find more joy in the task of growing human in the family when we recognize the ballet. Sometimes the dance is pure play—the tumbling of puppies, the sudden "let's pretend," or the more sedate play that has boundaries and rules. Sometimes the dance is wary. Sometimes it is agonizing.

Family therapists use choreography to enable deeply alienated married couples to see the dynamics of their own disrupted relationships. In the choreography of conflict, discrepancies between conscious and unconscious intent become blinding illuminations. Mostly, however, the family dance is just the choreography of the reserved life, of all the leftover inexpressibles from hours of duty out there in the social web. And always, the family dance is the Tao, the mirroring of the divine order, however imperfectly. We teeter back and forth between the created and the uncreated in the task of family growth.

Time Binding

When all is changing, where do we take hold? Only the present is secure. Tomorrow is scary. But the family binds tomorrow to the present and the past, for there is usually more than one generation. For a child, a parent is tomorrow, and a grandparent is day-after-tomorrow, even while telling the stories of yesterday and day-before-yesterday. For a parent, a child is both yesterday and tomorrow—the remembered past and the hoped-for future. The family is a living embodiment of the great Wheel of Life, and birth and death are never far apart.

Each of us relearns all the roles of the entire life span each day. In the larger society, we can often escape acknowledgments of the fact that those older and younger than ourselves have entered the time stream at a different point, and see different realities. In the family, we cannot ignore the vastly different memory stocks of each member, and the different forecasts and images of possible futures. Families cannot live in the present alone, as societies sometimes pretend to do. Past and future sit daily at the dinner table.

When life spaces are shared, when the I-remember and the I-hope enter into dialogue, each person gains a sense of ongoing social process, of anchoring in larger purposes. When three generations are present in a family, one of them is bound to be revolutionary. Storytelling bridges the generational gaps in ideology. Without storytelling, there can be no time binding, no coherence between past and future. The women's movement would not have had to be re-created in the 1960s if there had been better intergenerational transmission of its existence a hundred years ago. Similarly, the strategies of the world peace movement would not have had to be reinvented in each generation since the 1820s if the stories had been better told from parent to child.

Birth and death time-bind too. The new infant commits the family to the next century. Parental imagination must sometimes play there. Meeting death with a loved one, we travel both ways. We take meaning from their own final encounter—"the last of life, for which the first was made." Past and future become one.

Family Healing

Family acts of healing are also time binding, as they give glimpses into the most inward of our life spaces across generations. The child or teenager who comforts a distraught mother in a deep sorrow, or helps a defeated father face despair—such role reversals are rarely noted but occur almost universally in families. We expect parents to nurture children, but forget that children also nurture parents. Even the fact that children often nurse sick and temporarily bedridden parents is by a twist of the social memory simply forgotten. Each act of healing becomes a part of the personality of both healer and healed, a part of each person's future. Oriented to medical technology as we have been, we overlook the fact that the most significant experiences with illness and healing are family experiences, with son or daughter, brother or sister, mother or father as caregiver. The medical profession is now belatedly noting that healing is more in the hands of the person who is ill, and that person's family, than the hands of doctors, nurses, and hospitals. Yet restoring to families a sense of their own healing function will not be easy, since they have so long been taught to distrust their ability to handle illness. Confidence in an ability to heal in the family is confidence in a capacity for social healing.

Conflict Maturing

If the family is the space in the social web where individuality can be nurtured, then the family must also be the site of intense conflict, for individuals infringe on one another in intimate settings. We all know from our own experience that this is so. Maturing in the capacity to handle conflict is one of the most discussed and least understood aspects of family life. We give a lot of lip service to conflict management and conflict avoidance—we have workshops on how to "fight fair"—but with little understanding of conflict maturing. Thus a husband-wife conflict is either "managed" (usually through verbal communication) or avoided; if neither is possible, it is often recommended that the marriage be ended. It is not thinkable to live with deep-seated, unresolvable conflicts. Similarly, parent-child differences are to be handled with good communication, and are supposed to be manageable if enough skill is exercised.

While conflict avoidance, conflict management, "fighting" skills, and communication skills are all very important and legitimate approaches to family conflict, they must not substitute for an understanding of the basic process of conflict maturing. Precisely because family life at its best enhances the process of individuation in each member, profound differences in attitudes, values, and life perspectives may develop over the years between adults, and between adults and children. Such differences should not be considered an attack on family wholeness, but rather an affirmation of the individuality of each member of the whole. There is a terrible paradox in the love of husband and wife for each other, and the love of parents and children for each other. The more the family members have loved and shared in the past, the more intolerable differences can appear, precisely because we have been used to seeing things in the same way. Some terrible betrayal must have taken place! What has happened to the cherished common values? Rarely have they completely disappeared. More often, they have come to be interpreted so differently that their surface commonality disappears.

I have found a metaphor that has been most helpful in understanding this phenomenon between husband and wife. Two young trees are planted close together in common soil at marriage. They send down roots together, and feed on many of the same nutrients. But as they grow taller and older some of the roots shoot out in different directions, away from each other, seeking mutually alien soil. Nevertheless, the older, original roots stay intertwined. The trees also grow above ground. Many of their branches intertwine and shape each other in the happy embrace of shared space. Heaven continues to beckon, for a tree must "lift its leafy arms above," and a sense of lifting and reaching is shared. But these trees are not only growing toward each other; they are growing in all directions. Like the roots, some of the branches stretch far away from the common center, and breathe a mutually alien air. Each tree is in itself whole and individual and growing according to its inner design, yet shaped on the one side by its partner, on the other by the outside world.

In a profound sense the two trees are one, yet separate. Uprooting and transplanting would be excruciatingly difficult; one or both trees might be killed. Seen by an outsider, the trees can be admired both in their togetherness and their separateness. I will not push that metaphor further. You must make of it what you will. I will simply add that a family is a small grove of trees planted close together. Each new young tree that grows from parent seed also experiences this mingling of roots and branches, and the separateness of new growth away from the center.

The more we are faithful to our togetherness *and* our separateness, which is what the inherent contradictions of the family Tao ensure, the more pain we may feel. Pain can either be seen as something to be avoided, which is what our society generally teaches, or it can be seen as a signal of growth. It is seeing pain as a signal of growth that makes the conflict-maturing process possible. Each element of the conflict can be allowed to take its own shape, and then, by stepping back, this impossible, warring configuration can be seen as an embodiment of Creation. What stands there is in the hand of God. The letting be of the other is crucial. In the facing of contradiction is growth. In fleeing it—though there are times when we do flee, and perhaps should flee—we shrink at least a little.

While we must acknowledge and face contradictions, we do not have to flagellate ourselves with them. Contradictions are gulfs, and most gulfs can be bridged for purposes of daily life. The bridge of shared memories is always available. It may seem like a flimsy bridge, but it is not. We pull it out all the time in family life. The "remember when" sessions of family reunions are but intensified versions of what we do daily with our stranger-loved ones in word, glance, and gesture—evoking the familiar to smooth over the unfamiliar.

Nevertheless, the hard edges of contradictions remain, and for all our skill and good will we will trip on them again and again. This is why the capacity for conflict maturing between adults and children is as necessary for family well-being as is the capacity to love. The maturing of differences is so important because, as I have said earlier, the family provides the only space in the social web for the fostering of our individuality. Outside the family we are accepted and supported in parts and pieces, but mainly we must trim our edges to fit each social situation. When the family functions as I have been suggesting here, the *dance* permits each person to grow without trimming the edges. The choreography of movement ensures a minimum of bumping.

But oh, the discipline of learning to dance! This is not generally the free-flowing spontaneous movement you or I might break into alone in a meadow, although sometimes it is indeed that. It is instead the stretching of all kinds of muscles; it is learning to move the body in ways that it cannot move spontaneously. In family interaction, we must be able to move in all kinds of ways that are not sponta-

neous to us. The "love God and do as you please" of St.
Augustine and the effortless nondoing of Chuang Tzu are
based on a lifetime of disciplining unaccustomed muscles.

Taoist stories are full of hints about this kind of discipline.
One of my favorites, found in Thomas Merton's *The Way
of Chuang Tzu,* is "Cutting Up an Ox":

> Prince Wen Hui's cook
> Was cutting up an ox.
> Out went a hand,
> Down went a shoulder,
> He planted a foot,
> He pressed with a knee,
> The ox fell apart
> With a whisper,
> The bright cleaver murmured
> Like a gentle wind.
> Rhythm! Timing!
> Like a sacred dance,
> Like "The Mulberry Grove,"
> Like ancient harmonies!

The cook explains to the Prince that:

> A good cook needs a new chopper
> Once a year—he cuts.
> A poor cook needs a new one
> Every month—he hacks!

> "I have used this same cleaver
> Nineteen years.
> It has cut up
> A thousand oxen.
> Its edge is as keen
> As if newly sharpened.

> "There are spaces in the joints;
> The blade is thin and keen:
> When this thinness
> Finds that space
> There is all the room you need!
> It goes like a breeze!"

A lifetime of training has enabled him to find the secret opening, the hidden space, between the resisting body joints. "I cut through no joint, chop no bone," says the cook. The cook's unerring feel for the secret openings in that tightly constructed animal, the ox, symbolizes for me the skill of disciplined yet relaxed interaction that makes family togetherness an experience of tenderness and ease rather than of pain. We have so much tension and tightness in the family joints, yet the spaces to pass through are there if we know how to find them.

I have not found Taoist stories that apply this teaching directly to family life. The teachings of Taoism should not be confused with the teachings of Confucianism, which talk about "how to be a husband" and "how to be a daughter." The free flow of the dance of Tao is missing from these ritualized conceptions of family behavior. Releasing this free flow into the creative core of society through family life may be something that has been reserved for our own times. The key to our enduring ability to envision the good, and our enduring inability to produce enough goodness in human behavior to change our social course from a violent to a nonviolent one, must lie at least as much in the family as in our capacity for social design. Crafts are learned not by textbooks but by apprenticeships. And so it remains for our generation to rediscover and transmit an ancient unsung craft, one not to be found in the Great Books—the craft of family life.

We do not love one another in families simply because we ought to, or because we have developed competence in loving, though indeed we "ought" to love one another and indeed loving improves with the practice of love. We love one another beyond reason and beyond design, at the far side of hurt and anger, because there is an order of loving in the Creation of which we are a part. It is this order of loving in Creation which the Peaceable Kingdom passage in Isaiah describes:

> The wolf shall dwell with the lamb, and the leopard shall lie down
> with the kid, and the calf and the young lion and the fatling

together, and a little child shall lead them.

    The cow and the bear shall feed; their young ones shall lie down together; and the lion shall eat straw like the ox.

    And the sucking child shall play over the hole of the asp, and the weaned child shall put his hand on the adder's den.

    They shall not hurt or destroy in all my holy mountain; for the earth shall be full of the knowledge of the Lord as the waters cover the sea *(Isaiah 11:6-9)*.

This is a parable of family life, as well as a parable of nations. It is rationally improbable, yet we recognize this scene. It is familiar, with a familiarity that goes beyond simply having heard the words often. We can love and trust the "beasts" who are our parents, our children, our brothers and sisters, because we are bonded at another level. We are bonded in the knowledge of God, which is also the love of God. The Bible tells us over and over again that the most intimate bond of parent to child, of brother to sister, is also the bond that unites us with the rest of Creation. "They shall not hurt or destroy in all my holy mountain; for the earth shall be full of the knowledge of the Lord as the waters cover the sea."

None of the great religions has known how to teach about the knowledge and love of Creation without using the metaphor of the family. The teaching of love has always involved a paradoxical yoking of the cosmic and the particular. God so loved the *world* that he gave his *son*. Julian of Norwich writes:

> And so I saw that God rejoices that he is our Father, and God rejoices the he is our Mother, and God rejoices that he is our true spouse, and that our soil is his beloved wife. And Christ rejoices that he is our brother, and Jesus rejoices that he is our saviour.

When Lady Julian refers to God as parent and spouse, she is not diminishing the divine to cozy human levels. In Julian's mystic perception, our own spousehood and parenthood, so tangible and earthy, also partake of the Uncreated and thus lead us to the heart of Creation. Creation is always an act of love. To the extent that the family is faithful to its nature and tasks, it is alive with love. But

we are not very good at practicing love on each other, not
without a relationship with our divine parent, our divine
spouse. With God's help, the family is the best practice
ground for love that we have.

Whether or not we become good enough at the practice
of love in the family to warrant trying ourselves out in
relationship with other human beings, we do plunge across
the family-community boundary very early in life. From
our first experiences of co-creating a micro-world with God
and each other in the family, we stumble out into neighborhood and community, and practice co-creating community
there long before we can spell the words. As large-scale
bureaucracies falter, neighborhood innovation and community self-help enterprises can inject a stream of fresh
capabilities into the heavily stressed social order. Of course,
the tasks that lie before us are out of all proportion to our
abilities. How are we to create viable new local community
structures to replace the frayed structures of industrial cen-
tralism, in a dynamic context of world neighborhood,
world need, world service? Yet that is what we must do,
and it is the high calling of family life to prepare us for
this kind of co-creation.

Kenneth Boulding wrote a sonnet for a Quaker wedding
many years ago which describes this calling simply and
powerfully, and I would like to close with his words:

> Put off the garb of woe, let mourning cease;
> Today we celebrate with solemn mirth,
> The planting in the ravaged waste of earth
> Of one small plot of heaven, a Home of peace,
> Where love unfeigned shall rule, and bring increase,
> And pure eternal joy shall come to birth
> And grow, and flower, that neither drought nor dearth
> Shall wither, till the Reaper brings release.
>
> Guard the ground well, for it belongs to God;
> Root out the hateful and the bitter weed,
> And from the harvest of thy Heart's good seed
> The hungry shall be fed, the naked clad,
> And love's infection, leaven-like, shall spread
> Till all creation feeds from heavenly bread.

Bibliography

Barbour, Hugh. *Margaret Fell Speaking*. Pendle Hill Pamphlet 206. Wallingford: Pendle Hill Publications, 1976.

Benedict, Ruth. "Continuities and Discontinuities in Cultural Conditioning." *Psychiatry* 1 (1935): 161-67.

Boulding, Elise. "Who Are These Women? Report on Research on the New Women's Peace Movement," in *Behavioral Science and Human Survival*. Edited by M. Schwebel. Palo Alto: Science and Behavior Books, Inc., 1965.

Boulding, Elise M. *From a Monastery Kitchen*. New York: Harper & Row, 1976.

Boulding, Elise. *The Underside of History: A View of Women Through Time*. Boulder: Westview Press, 1976.

Boulding, Elise. "The Child and Nonviolent Social Change," in *Strategies Against Violence: Design for Nonviolent Personal Relationships, Communities and International Relationships*. Edited by Israel Charny. Boulder: Westview Press, 1978.

Boulding, Elise. *Children's Rights and the Wheel of Life*. New Brunswick: Transaction Books, 1979.

Boulding, Elise. "The Labor of U.S. Farm Women: A Knowledge Gap." *Sociology of Work and Occupations* 7 (Aug. 1980).

Boulding, Elise. "The Nurture of Adults by Children in Family Settings," in *Research in the Interweave of Social Roles*. Edited by Helen Z. Lopata. Greenwich: Jai Press, 1980.

Boulding, Kenneth E. *There Is A Spirit: The Nayler Sonnets*. Nyack: Fellowship Press, 1945.

Brinton, Howard. *The Nature of Quakerism*. Pendle Hill Pamphlet 47. Wallingford: Pendle Hill Publications, 1962.

Brother Lawrence. *The Practice of the Presence of God*. Springfield: Templegate Publishers, 1974.

Brutz, Judy. "How Precious Is Our Testimony?" *Friends Journal* 30 (Oct. 1, 1984): 8-9.

Brutz, Judy. "Parable and Transforming Power Among Friends." (Address given at Illinois and Ohio Valley Yearly Meetings, 1985.)

Brutz, Judy and B.B. Ingoldsby. "Conflict Resolution in Quaker Families." *Journal of Marriage and the Family* 46 (Feb. 1984): 21-26.

Brutz, Judy and Craig Allen. "Religious Commitment, Peace Activism and Marital Violence in Quaker Families." *Journal of Marriage and the Family* 48 (Aug. 1986): 491-502.

Buber, Martin. *I and Thou*. Translated by Ronald Gregor Smith. New York: Charles Scribner's Sons, 1958.

Burns, Scott. *Home, Inc.: The Hidden Wealth and Power of the American Household*. Garden City: Doubleday & Co., 1975.

Castillo, Fortunato. *Aggression and Hostility in Quaker Families*. (1974 Rufus Jones Lecture.) Philadelphia: Friends General Conference, 1974.

Clarkson, Thomas. *Portraiture of Quakerism*. 3 vols. New York: Samuel Stansburg, 1806.

De la Mare, Walter. *Early One Morning in the Spring*. London: Faber & Faber, 1935.

Elgin, Duane. *Voluntary Simplicity*. New York: William Morrow and Company 1981.

Evans, William and Thomas Evans, eds. *The Friends Library: comprising Journals, Doctrinal Treatises, and other writings of members of the Religious Society of Friends*. 14 vols. Philadelphia: Joseph Rakestraw, 1837-1850.

Ferguson, Marilyn. *The Aquarian Conspiracy: Personal and Social Transformation in the 1980s*. New York: J.P. Tarcher, 1981.

Flexner, Helen Thomas. *Quaker Childhood*. New Haven: Yale University Press, 1940.

Fry, Elizabeth. *Memoir of the Life of Elizabeth Fry*. Montclair: Patterson Smith, 1974.

Gandhi, Mohandas K. *Autobiography: The Story of My Experiments With Truth.* New York: Dover Publications, 1983.

Goertzel, Mildred and Victor. *Cradles of Eminence.* Boston: Little, Brown & Co., 1962.

Goertzel, Mildred, Victor Goertzel, and Theodore Goertzel. *33 Eminent Personalities.* San Francisco: Jossey-Bass, 1978.

Harvey, William Fryer. *We Were Seven.* London: Constable & Co., 1936.

Jones, Rufus M. *Finding the Trail of Life.* New York: Macmillan Co.,1950.

Julian of Norwich. *Julian of Norwich: Showings.* Edited by Edmund Colledge et al. New York: Paulist Press, 1978.

Klingberg, Göte. "A Study of the Religious Experience in Children from 9 to 13 Years of Age." Translated by Elise Boulding. *Religious Education* 54 (May 1959): 211-216.

Kurz, Demie. "Violence and Inequality in the Family." *Friends Journal* 30 (Oct. 1, 1984): 10-12.

LeClercq, Jean. *Love and Learning and the Desire for God.* Translated by Catherine Misrahi. New York: Fordham University Press, 1960.

Mace, David. "Violence in Quaker Families." *Friends Journal* 30 (Oct. 1, 1984): 7-8.

McGinnis, James and Katherine. *Parenting for Peace and Justice.* New York: Orbis Books, 1981.

Merton, Thomas. *The Way of Chuang Tzu.* New York: New Directions, 1969.

Moen, Elizabeth, Elise Boulding, Jane Lilleydahl and Rise Palm. *Women and the Social Costs of Economic Development: Two Colorado Case Studies.* Boulder: Westview Press, 1981.

Naisbitt, John. *Megatrends.* New York: Warner Books, 1981.

Nigg, Walter. *The Heretics.* New York: Alfred A. Knopf, 1962.

O'Neill, George and Nena O'Neill. *Open Marriage: A New Lifestyle for Couples.* New York: M. Evans & Co., 1984.

Orwell, George. *1984*. London: Secker & Warburg, 1949.

Penn, William. *Some Fruits of Solitude.* New York: S. Bucklen & Co., 1901.

Reeves, Marjorie. *The Influence of Prophecy in the Later Middle Ages: A Study in Joachimism.* Oxford: Clarendon Press, 1969.

Riesman, David. *Individualism Reconsidered and Other Essays.* Glencoe: Free Press, 1954.

Ruddick, Sara. "Preservative Love and Military Destruction: Reflections on Mothering and Peace," in *Mothering and Feminist Theory.* Edited by Joyce Tribilcott. Totona: Littlefield, Adams, 1985.

Schumacher, E.F. *Small is Beautiful.* New York: Harper and Row, 1973.

Sharp, Gene. *Transarmament.* New York: Institute for World Order, 1981.

Tanquerey, Adolphe. *The Spiritual Life: A Treatise on Ascetical and Mystical Theology.* Translated by Herman Branderis. Desdée & Co., 1930.

Tauler, John. *Spiritual Conferences.* Translated by Eric and Jane Colledge. Rockford: TAN Books & Publishers, 1979.

Tough, Alan. *The Adult's Learning Projects.* Toronto: Institute for Studies in Education, 1979.

Turner, Victor. *The Ritual Process: Structure and Antistructure.* Chicago: Aldine Publishing Co., 1969.

Underhill, Evelyn. *Mysticism: A Study in the Nature and Development of Man's Spiritual Consciousness.* New York: E.P. Dutton, 1961.

Wahl, Jan. *How the Children Stopped the Wars.* New York: Avon Books, 1983.

Wells, H.G. *The Outline of History.* London: Cassell & Co., 1920.

Wells, H.G. *Experiment in Autobiography: Discoveries and Conclusions of a Very Ordinary Brain.* New York: MacMillan Co., 1934.

Woolman, John. *The Journal and Major Essays of John Woolman.* Edited by Phillips P. Moulton. New York: Oxford University Press, 1971.

Whyte, William H. *Organization Man.* New York: Simon & Schuster, 1956.

Index

Library of Congress Cataloging-in-Publication Data

Boulding, Elise.
    One small plot of heaven : reflections on family life by a Quaker
sociologist / Elise Boulding.
        p.   cm.
    Bibliography: p. 219
    Includes index.
    ISBN 0-87574-912-7 : $12.50
    1. Family. 2. Quakers—Family relationships. 3. Family—
Religious life. 4. Boulding, Elise. 5. Sociologists—United
States—Biography. 6. Quakers—United States—Biography.
I. Title.
HQ503.B54 1989
306.85—dc20   89-16082
                                                                              CIP